Scats
and
Tracks
of the

Great Plains

SCATS AND TRACKS SERIES

Scats
and
Tracks
of the

Great Plains

A Field Guide to the Signs of Seventy Wildlife Species

James C. Halfpenny, PhD

Illustrated by Todd Telander

GUILFORD, CONNECTICUT
HELENA, MONTANA

AN IMPRINT OF THE GLOBE PEQUOT PRESS

ΛFALCON GUIDE®

Maps created by James Halfpenny, PhD © Morris Book Publishing, LLC

Library of Congress Cataloging-in-Publication Data
Halfpenny, James C.
  Scats and tracks of the Great Plains : a field guide to the signs of seventy wildlife species / James C. Halfpenny; illustrated by Todd Telander. — 1st ed.
       p. cm. — (A Falconguide) (Scats and tracks series)
  Includes bibliographical references.
  ISBN-13: 978-0-7627-4232-5
  ISBN-10: 0-7627-4232-1
  1. Animal tracks—Great Plains. I. Bruchac, James. II. Title.
  QL768.H3544 2006
  596.0978—dc22

                                        2006026128

Manufactured in the United States of America
First Edition/First Printing

To Marvin Miller, Boy Scout leader, for his faith in a young scout and for all he taught the youth of Wyo-Braska Council and Laramie Peak Scout Camp.

To Bill Desmarais, teacher extraordinary, for all he has shared with his students, especially at the National Wildlife Federation Summits.

To Diann, my alpha partner, ursophile, and tracking friend, for all her loving support and help.

–JH

Contents

Acknowledgments

First and foremost, I wish to thank all my students for their years of questions and help, but most of all for the time we've shared tracking and studying in the field. I also wish to thank Lee Fitzhugh, Larry Marlow, Murie Museum, Teton Science School, and Terry McEneany (Yellowstone National Park) for his help with bird tracks.

JH

Introduction

In the late 1970s, the era of watchable wildlife arrived in the United States. Baby boomers wanted to turn to and experience the outdoors. Television brought wildlife closer than ever. Bird-watching thrived. Now more than ever, millions of people want to watch wild animals. Wildlife are not always easy to find and observe, though. Finding tracks and signs is an exciting alternative to actually seeing the animals. Trackable wildlife adds another dimension to the outdoor experience. Todd and I wish to share that dimension, the joy of reading stories written in the soil and snow.

Upwards of ten books on tracking have been written in the United States during each decade of the twentieth century. Most are general, covering the United States or all of North America. In *Scats and Tracks of the Great Plains,* we focus on one biogeographic region, with details about the region's most common or characteristic species of mammals, birds, reptiles, and amphibians. (We have included a few rare species because of their particular interest or significance in a region. For example, what a coup it would be to document a swift fox, or a pocket mouse, or a horned lizard.) We've intentionally limited the number of species covered in order to keep the information manageable. This guide is small, allowing you to carry it in a pack or pocket and use it frequently.

As your knowledge and interest in tracking grows, you may want to find additional information and help. Key references are listed in Selected Reading. For a more detailed investigation of tracking, I recommend my book *A Field Guide to Mammal Tracking in North America* (1986, Johnson Publishing, Boulder, Colorado), and titles by Olaus Murie, Mark Elbroch, Louise R. Forrest, and Paul Rezendes.

My organization will, in computer parlance, provide interactive access to expand your tracking background. A Naturalist's World (ANW), directed by myself, is an ecologically oriented company dedicated to providing educational programs and materials reflecting the natural history of North America. Diann Thompson and I run the daily business, teach classes, and lead programs. Our on-site classes provide hands-on experience and in-depth information about animals, their tracks, and the ecology of their environments. In addition to tracking classes, our field programs cover the behavior of bears, wolves, winter ecology, the northern lights, and alpine ecology. ANW also provides books, videos, slide shows, and computer programs for self-study and as teaching and field aids. You can check out ANW on the Internet at www.track nature.com. Class schedules, product information, and information about ANW can be obtained from P.O. Box 989, Gardiner, MT 59030, phone (406) 848–9458, or on the Web at www.tracknature.com and www.tracking animals.net.

Keep on tracking!

—James C. Halfpenny

About Tracking

Tracking is for everyone—beginner and expert, young and old. The fun of nature's challenge is solving the mystery written in the trail. Prepare yourself by learning the background and basics of tracking before exercising your skills in the field.

Field notes and preserving tracks

To the natural history detective, the track and trail are things of great beauty and significance. They tell part of the story of an animal's life. Tracks and trails deserve to be preserved, both to increase your knowledge and as a record you can share with others. Preservation is commonly made in the form of written notes, casts, or photographs.

Perhaps the most important item in the naturalist's tool kit is the field notebook. Field notes can jog the memory and facilitate better retention of knowledge. The notes can be analyzed later and can be preserved as records of chance encounters. Writing good field notes is an art form and a science in itself. Field notes are a source of pride when shown to others and may gain recognition for recording rare and unusual events. And need I mention how quickly memories, especially for details, fade when not preserved?

While great and complex systems have been designed for complete and accurate records, there are really but three requirements for the tracker: ruler, paper, and pen. With these, every trail becomes a record for later analysis and sharing. We cannot emphasize enough the importance of enhancing your tracking experience by keeping notes to which you can later refer!

A simple 3-by-5-inch notebook and a 6-inch ruler are adequate to get started. Use a pencil or a pen that won't run if your notes get wet. To facilitate taking notes, A Naturalist's World produces a waterproof notebook that contains information about footprint groups, gaits, and how to track; data sheets for recording information; and English and metric rulers imprinted on the back cover. See the Introduction for contact information for A Naturalist's World.

Tracks may also be preserved by photographing and making casts. Good photographs can be made by any modern camera that can take a good close-up. When taking pictures, try to fill the viewfinder with the footprint. Get as close as possible. Always include a ruler or some other object in the photo to provide a sense of scale. Avoid using hats, gloves, hands, or objects without a straight edge; round edges do not lend themselves to making accurate measurements from a photo. To avoid distortion, take the photograph from directly above the track, shooting straight down. Also, step back and take photographs of the trail to show the footprints that were photographed close-up. Fast films (ASA of 200 or higher) are generally best because tracks are often found in dark places, especially ground surfaces. Modern digital cameras take excellent photographs that can easily be e-mailed to others.

Plaster casts are the old standby for preserving tracks. We suggest a casting kit that includes a one-gallon (four-liter) wide-mouthed plastic jar with a screw lid for carrying dry plaster, a narrow spatula, a plastic mixing cup such as those sold for medium-size drinks, paper for wrapping and transporting the finished cast, and a plastic sack for cleanup. A bottle of water may be needed if water is not available on site. Two pounds of plaster will make at least four coyote-size track casts.

Purchase plaster from a lumberyard or hardware store, as prices will be more reasonable than at a drugstore or hobby shop. Almost any plaster will work, including plaster of paris, hydrocal, ultracal, or hydrostone. Avoid getting plaster for wallboard or patching compound, however. These plasters are formulated to be slightly flexible on walls and do not get hard enough for casts. Also avoid PolyPlasters as they do not set well when the temperature is cooler than 50 degrees Fahrenheit.

Two factors are critical to preventing casts from breaking: thickness and density. In the field, thickness is assured by building a wall around the track to contain the plaster. Natural objects such as twigs, stones, and dirt may be used to make a retaining wall 0.25 to 0.5 inch (0.6 to 1.3 cm) above the track. Alternatively, walls in the form of plastic strips cut from milk cartons or other plastic containers may be taken to the field. Proper density is assured by mixing two parts of plaster to one part of water by volume (read instructions on plaster container) to create a mixture similar in consistency to thick pancake batter or a milk shake.

Place your spatula close to the track and pour onto the spatula to break the fall of the plaster into the footprint. Working quickly, so the plaster does not set and become too thick, gently pour the plaster first into the fine detailed areas of the footprint and then the rest of the print. Finally, pour the plaster to an appropriate depth (inside the retaining wall) to keep the cast from breaking. Vibrating the spatula up and down across the top of the plaster will cause it to settle evenly and create a smooth back for the cast.

Allow the plaster to dry for thirty minutes, or as long as is recommended on the plaster package. Gently pick the plaster up by digging your fingers under opposite sides of the cast, and turn the cast over onto one hand.

Now wash off the dirt by rubbing the cast with your fingertips under the flowing water of a stream or a hose. Do not wash the cast in a sink as plaster may clog the drain. Let the cast continue to cure for several days in a warm, dry environment. If you need to transport it, wrap the cast in paper. Never wrap the cast in plastic as trapped moisture may cause it to crumble.

While special techniques are needed for dust and snow, this procedure will allow casting in many situations. Remember, carry a plastic garbage bag and always clean up your mess. No sign of your plaster should remain to reduce the experience of others who happen by later.

Scats and bird pellets

Scats and bird pellets (also called cough pellets or castings) are often helpful for identifying an animal or completing the story written in the trail. Scats and pellets help identify not only what the animal was eating, but who the animal was. However, it should be noted that scats and pellets won't help you identify an animal with as much certainty as tracks will. Many animals make similar scats and pellets that are difficult to tell apart.

The scats of many carnivores are very similar, especially when the diet is mostly meat. Size alone does not provide a definitive answer because of the wide range of diameters produced within a species and even by a single member of a species. For example, fox produce scats ranging in size from 0.3 to 0.8 inch (0.8 to 2.0 cm), coyotes produce scats from 0.5 to 1.3 inches (1.3 to 3.3 cm), and wolves produce scats from 0.5 to 1.5 inches (1.3 to 3.8 cm), and we all know how our own scat varies in size and shape. When judging size, consider both the total quantity of scat and the size of individual pieces. Moist food produces slimmer scats, while fibrous diets produce wider scats.

Given these cautions, scat shapes can be used to identify general groups of animals (see page xix). Spherical
shapes flattened top to bottom are deposited by members
of the rabbit order. Elongate spheres are deposited by
rodents and shrews, and at larger sizes by deer and their
relatives. Long, thick cords are deposited by dogs, bears,
and raccoons. Dog scats typically have tapered ends,
while those from bears and raccoons are blunt. Cats also
produce thick cords with blunt ends, but they tend to be
constricted or even broken into short segments. Cords
that loop back on themselves are produced by members of
the weasel family.

Birds, in general, produce long, thin cords or shapeless, semiliquid excretions. Reptiles and amphibians may
produce small elongate spheres or long, thin cords.
White, nitrogenous urine deposits, found only on the
scats of birds, reptiles, and amphibians, separate them
from mammal scats.

Scats may be confused with cough pellets. Many bird
groups, including owls, raptors, crows, ravens, jays, mag-
pies, gulls, herons, storks, flycatchers, and kingfishers,
produce cough pellets in addition to scats. Birds pass
digestive juices through what they have eaten to remove
the nutrients. Hair, bones, beaks, claws, and other nondi-
gestible parts accumulate in the gizzard (anterior portion
of stomach), are compressed, and are coughed up as pellets. Bone and hair remnants in the pellet are easy to
identify and tell much about the bird's feeding habits and
even the habitats it frequents.

Pellets are grayish in color and are spherical or long
and tapered at both ends. When fresh, they are covered by
mucus and appear dark black. Pellets are found mainly at
roosting sites and nests, and occasionally at feeding areas.
They are deposited singly, but many may accumulate

beneath a tree where a bird is roosting, nesting, or perching. Nitrogenous scat deposits on the ground or twigs may help verify an object as a pellet. The diameter of the throat determines the maximum diameter of the pellet. In general, large birds produce larger pellets. Shape and diameter allow one to distinguish to some degree between species.

cough pellet

Birds generally produce two pellets per day and regurgitate just before taking flight. The time of day when feeding occurred may affect the sample of food items. For example, owls tend to feed on mammals that come out only at night, while hawks feed on animals that are out during the daylight hours.

Anatomy and footprint nomenclature

The feet of mammals, birds, reptiles, and amphibians are anatomically complex, and that complexity shows in their footprints. Knowing something of the anatomy of their feet will aid in footprint identification and interpreting trails.

The toes of all animals are numbered from the inside of the foot out (the inside of the foot being the side closest to the animal). Therefore, in humans and other mammals, the thumb or big toe (if present) is number 1 and the little finger or little toe is number 5. In birds, toe 1 (if present) points backward.

Over evolutionary time, toes of animals have become reduced in size or have disappeared altogether. In cats and dogs, toe 1 is absent or reduced to a small toe called a dewclaw. In deer, elk, sheep, and similar mammals, toe 1 is absent and toes 2 and 5 are reduced and form dewclaws. Toes 3 and 4, the clouts, form the cloven hoof. In

Shapes of scats

Spheres

Rabbits and their
relatives

rabbit

Spheres, elongate

Rodents, shrews,
deer, and their
relatives

woodrat

shrew

elk

Cords, long and thick

Wolves, bears,
raccoons, and their
relatives

coyote

bear

raccoon

Cords, thick and often constricted

Mountain lions and
their relatives

mountain lion

Cords, often folded

Weasels and their
relatives

mink

Cords, long and thin, often with nitrogenous deposits

Birds, reptiles, and amphibians

Canada goose

lizard

pronghorn antelope, toes 1, 2, and 5 are absent. In birds, toe 5 is absent and toe 1 is often reduced and occasionally is absent. In the amphibians covered here, toe 1 has been lost from the front foot.

Track measurements

To more accurately determine the animal's foot size from its tracks, mountain lion researchers Fjelline and Mansfield (1989) developed the minimum outline method of measuring tracks.

Place your hand on a hard surface, a table for instance. Note the contact area of your hand with that surface. If your hand went no deeper into that surface, your handprint would have only one size: the minimum outline. If your hand were to sink deeper into the surface—as it would if the surface were, say, mud—it would create a series of variable outlines, each larger than the one before, as the mud flowed around the curved surface of your hand. All footprints have a minimum outline, but only prints that sink into a surface have variable outlines.

Note that while the variable outline of a footprint may only be several millimeters wider than the minimum outline, those few millimeters have a large visual effect. The human eye sees area, and area increases with the square of a linear measurement. In short, a few millimeters of width adds a lot of area to a footprint.

The minimum outline size does not change for different surfaces and therefore provides a standard for comparison among surfaces. And though one animal may leave many sizes of footprints depending on surface, slope, and speed, there is only one minimum outline for every footprint that animal might leave. The minimum outline measurement is the only constant and consistent size in tracking.

To measure the minimum outline, study the bottom of a print. The *break point* where the rounded pad turns upward is the edge of the minimum outline. Use this edge to measure tracks. Assigning the break point is a subjective judgment and no two people will always mark it at exactly the same point. However, testing has shown that an individual tracker using the minimum outline method can reduce personal variation in measurement and that groups of trackers using this method will also become more consistent in their measurement of tracks. Remember the computer rule GIGO: garbage in, garbage out. You cannot get quality measurements from a bad track. Quality measurements are the tracker's goal, and using minimum outline methods greatly reduces over-exaggeration and variance in measurement.

cross section of footprint in ground

All measurements in this guide are minimum outline measurements.

The measurements in *Scats and Tracks of the Great Plains* are mostly averages gathered from years of tracking. Averages include only animals judged to be adult. However, it is important to remember the great size variation among animals. Every animal was small once in its life, and some never get big. Males are often substantially larger than females. Regional variations in mammal sizes also occur. For example, coyotes are smaller in the southwestern United States and larger in the northeastern part of the country. Their tracks vary accordingly. Therefore, a track in the field may be considerably larger or smaller than the measurements provided. Use track measurements only as a rough guideline, not as an absolute rule. Collect your own database of track measurements for your area.

Gaits and trails

Coordinated muscle movements result in the various gaits used by animals. In the simplest form, when moving on two legs (bipedal movement) an organism can *walk, run,* and *hop*. When moving on four legs (quadrupedal movement) an organism can *walk, trot, lope, gallop, bound,* and *pronk* (also called *stot*). Though other gaits exist, we will confine our discussion to these basic gaits. Each gait leaves a characteristic pattern that may be modified by changes in speed and body angle. The combination of footprints is called the *trail*. The bipedal walk and run and the quadrupedal walk and trot result in gaits that are *symmetrical*. The right side of the trail is a mirror image of the left side. The trail patterns for these gaits are the same, alternating right-left pattern, and they differ only by the stride being longer in the run and trot than it is in the walk. In the run and trot, the straddle, the distance from the right edge of the rightmost pad (see page xxxi) to the left edge of the leftmost pad, also tends to be narrower than it is in the walk.

walk   trot

Quadrupedal movement results in gaits that are *asymmetrical* (the right half of the trail is not always a mirror image of the left), including lope, gallop, bound, hop, and pronk. These gaits produce patterns that include all four footprints (two fronts, two hinds, two rights, and two lefts) in a group separated from the next group by a space where no footprints appear.

In *gallops,* the feet, front and rear, that move first (or *lead*) will determine whether the gallop will form a Z-shaped or C-shaped pattern. When the front and hind feet on the same side lead, the pattern takes on a Z shape. A right-front lead with a left-hind lead or vice versa results in a C-shaped pattern. Thus, there are four possible gallop patterns.

C-shaped gallop | Z-shaped gallop

large print–front feet
small print–rear feet

Bounds (also known as hops and jumps) are characterized by the synchronization of the hind feet; both strike the ground at the same time, side by side. The front feet strike the ground at a different

full bound | half bound

time than the hind feet. In a full bound, the front feet are synchronized and strike the ground side by side at the same time. In a half bound, only the hind feet are synchronized and the front feet hit the ground staggered. Animals that mostly use full bounds, also called hops, live in trees (tree squirrels and songbirds), whereas those that mostly use half bounds live on the ground (ground squirrels, rabbits, and grouse).

In a *pronk* (also called a *stot*), all four feet strike the ground at the same time, with the front feet side by side and forward of the hind feet, which are also side by side. The front

pronk

feet strike the ground forward of the hind feet. This gait is often used by deer to gain height and increase time in the air to look around. To increase peripheral vision, non-primate mammals have eyes placed toward the side of their heads, not flat on their face like humans. By turning sideways, a prey species can see what is pursuing it and where it needs to go to escape. The predator, by turning sideways, can see what it is chasing and where the rest of the predator pack is.

slow side trot

side gallop

Consequently, quadrupedal mammals have evolved to use all gaits while their body is turned to the side. These *side gaits* result when the animal's heavy head deviates from the line of travel and the body turns sideways. First, the front feet respond by moving toward the side of the trail where the head is. Then, as the head turns more, the hind feet move to the side away from the head. The greater the head movement, the greater the angle of the side gait. Common examples are the side trot and side gallop that are often used by canids. These are often called a dog trot or dog gallop.

An animal's size is also reflected in its gait patterns. When a mammal is walking with its normal gait, for example, the stride is 1.1 to 1.25 times larger than the distance from the hip to the shoulder joint. Using this crude relationship, body size can be judged from a walking stride. A 22-inch stride indicates a hip-to-shoulder length of 20 inches. Add to the hip-to-shoulder distance an estimate for the head length beyond the shoulder joint and an estimate of the rump length beyond the hip joint to get a total estimate of animal body length.

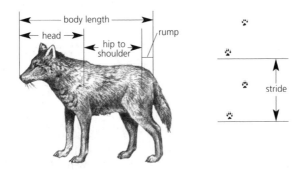

estimating mammal length from stride

Speed also modifies gait patterns in trails. There are three rules governing how pattern changes as speed changes:

1. As speed increases, the hind foot lands farther forward than the front footprint on the same side. Conversely, as speed decreases, the hind foot lands farther back in relation to the front footprint.

2. As speed increases, stride increases.

3. As speed increases, straddle usually decreases.

Speed changes are easily observed in quadrupedal walk and trot trail patterns. As speed increases, the hind footprint registers in front of the front print. This faster version of a walk is called an amble. The faster version of a trot doesn't have a name. When the animal slows to the point that the hind feet are registering behind the front prints, the animal may be stalking something. Trots are separated from walks by having a stride two or more times greater than the estimated hip-to-shoulder distance of an animal.

| 1 x 2 x 1 lope | 2 x 2 lope | 3 x 3 lope |

| walk (slower) | amble (faster) |

A slow version of the gallop is also recognizable. When a gallop slows to the point that one or more hind feet register behind the leading edge of the frontmost footprint in a group pattern, the gait is called a *lope*. The gait is still a gallop, it's just a slow gallop.

Trail measurements

The terms *stride, group, intergroup,* and *straddle* describe the size of an animal trail. The *stride* is measured from the point where a foot touches the ground surface to where the same point of the same foot next touches the surface, and consists of one group and one intergroup measurement. The *group* consists of all four footprints (two fronts, two hinds, two lefts, two rights), while the *intergroup* is the distance between groups. Gait patterns take their name from the configuration of the group. The stride provides an indication of size in a walking animal and an indication of relative speed for other gaits (see pages xxiv and xxv).

The *straddle* indicates the width of the trail and is measured from the outside rightmost pad of the outside right footprint of a group to the outside leftmost pad footprint of the same group. The outside edges of the trail are used because the inside of footprints overlap for many carnivore species. When measured from outside right to outside left, walking stride is an indicator of size.

Stride, group, and intergroup are all measured parallel to the trail, while the straddle is measured at right angles to the trail. Select a straight section of trail on level ground to measure. The slightest curve in the trail will distort the straddle measurement.

Glossary of terms

amble: a fast walk in which the hind footprint registers anterior to the front footprint. See illustration on page xxvi.

asymmetrical: not symmetrical; that is, one side is not a mirror image of the opposite side.

bound: a gait in which both hind feet strike the ground at the same time, side by side. If the front feet also land side by side, the motion is said to be a *full bound*. A *half bound* occurs when one front foot strikes the ground in front of the other. See illustration on page xxiii.

clout: term used to refer to toe 3 or toe 4 of the hoof. See illustration on page xxxii.

convergent toes: toes 2 and 4 of ducks, geese, and swans, which bend toward the foot axis, especially at the tips. Compare to *divergent* toes.

cord: See *scat shape*.

cough pellet: remnants of bones and hair coughed up by many bird species after feeding on prey.

dewclaw: toe that over evolutionary time has become reduced in size and raised on the leg, away from the other toes; for example, toe 1 in dogs and toes 2 and 5 in deer.

diagnostic: providing certain identification of an animal or its sign.

digit: one of the toes of an animal.

digital pad: See *pad*.

digitigrade: walking on the tips of the toes. Dogs and cats, for example, are digitigrade. Tracks left by digitigrade animals rarely show a sole. Compare to *plantigrade*.

distal webbing: See *webbing*.

divergent toes: toes that are straight or turn out from the *foot axis* at the tips, specifically toes 2 and 4 of seagulls. Compare to *convergent* toes.

foot axis: imaginary line down the center of the foot. It runs between toes 3 and 4 in deer and their relatives, and down toe 3 of other mammals. In birds, the foot axis also runs down toe 3.

fringe: webbing attached to a single toe. May have a smooth edge, known as a *simple fringe*

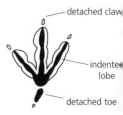

detached claw

indented lobe

detached toe

or *simple lobe,* or it may be wavy, in which case it is said to have *indented lobes.*

full bound: See *bound.*

gait: term for the type(s) of movement an animal uses when moving. Examples of gaits include *walk, amble, trot, bound,* and *gallop.* Gaits are defined by the mechanics of body movement, not by speed.

gallop: a gait in which hind feet move around the front feet and (usually) strike the ground in front of the front feet. Galloping forms distinct group patterns (two fronts, two hinds, two lefts, two rights) separated by an intergroup distance from the next set of four feet. Gallops fall into two basic patterns: Z-shaped and C-shaped.

group: a subunit of a *stride* including four footprints (two fronts and two hinds, and two lefts and two rights). The measure of the group plus the intergroup equals the measure of the stride.

half bound: See *bound.*

heel: portion of foot or track to the rear of digital and interdigital pads. In mammals, may be covered with hair, naked (without hair), or have one or more proximal pads. In reptiles and amphibians, may be textured with *tubercles.*

gallops

bounds

hop: synonymous with bound, often used in reference to *gaits* of rodents and rabbits.

indented lobe: See *fringe.*

interdigital pad: See *pad.*

length: of a track, the distance from front of toe *pads* to back of the interdigital pads, measured parallel to the *foot axis.* In mammal tracks, does not include claws. In bird tracks, does not include toe 1, but includes claws if they are attached and indistinguishable from toe pad.

line of travel: imaginary line on the ground over which the center of gravity of an animal passes.

lobe: See *fringe.*

lope: a slow *gallop,* in which at least one hind foot registers behind a front foot in a group of four footprints. See illustration on page xxvi.

mesial webbing: See *webbing*.

minimum outline: See pages xiii and xiv for extended discussion.

nipple-dimple: See *scat shape*.

outer toe angle: in birds, the angle between toes 2 and 4. In perching birds less than 90 degrees and in shorebirds greater than 120 degrees.

oval: See *scat shape*.

pad: hard, calluslike structure on the sole of an animal's foot. Each toe may have a digital pad. One or more interdigital pads are located directly to the rear of the toes, and one or more proximal pads may be located directly to the rear of the interdigital pads. In deer and their relatives, there is a single pad separated from the *wall* by the *subunguinis*. In birds, a metatarsal pad may occur directly under the leg bone.

plantigrade: walking on the soles of the foot. Raccoons, bears, and humans, for example, are plantigrade. The sole of the foot usually shows in the footprint. Compare to *digitigrade*.

pronk: a *gait* in which all four feet strike the ground simultaneously and directly below the body. The *group* pattern shows two front footprints ahead of the two hind prints. Also called a *stot*. See illustration on page xxiii.

proximal pad: See *pad*.

proximal webbing: See *webbing*.

rotatory gallop: a type of *gallop* that tends to form a C-shaped *group* pattern. See illustration on page xxiii.

run: a *gait* used when moving only on two legs. It differs from a *walk* in having a longer *stride*.

scat shape: *Cords* are long pieces of scat, typically four to ten times longer than the width. Ends may be blunt or tapered. *Ovals* are pieces of scat typically two to four times longer than wide and tapered at both ends. A *nipple-dimple*-shaped scat pellet has a point at one end and a depression at the other. See chart on page xix.

simple fringe, simple lobe: See *fringe*.

sole: bottom of an animal's foot. It may be covered with hair or naked, and may have one or more *pads* on it.

stot: See *pronk.*

straddle: the distance from the right edge of the rightmost pad to the left edge of the leftmost pad in a *trail.* Measured at right angles to the *line of travel.*

stride: the distance from the point where a foot touches the ground to the point where the same foot touches the ground again. Measured parallel to the *line of travel.* One stride is equal to a *group* plus an intergroup measurement.

subunguinis: the soft material under the nails of humans. In deer and their relatives, refers specifically to the soft material between the *pad* and *wall.*

symmetrical: having two sides, one the mirror image of the other side.

toe pad: See *pad.*

track: refers to an individual footprint. Some measurable characteristics include *length* and *width.*

track pattern: the gross visual image of the pattern of footprints on the ground. A repeating pattern of two prints separated from the next two is called two-by-two and written 2 x 2. Prints may also show patterns of 3 x 3, 4 x 4, and 1 x 2 x 1. These patterns are made during a *gallop* or a *bound.* A few of these patterns are illustrated on page xxvi.

trail: a series of footprints and associated sign that marks the passage of an animal. Some measurable characteristics include *stride* and *straddle.*

transverse gallop: a type of gallop that tends to form a Z-shaped group pattern. See illustration on page xxiii.

trot: a *gait* in which evenly spaced footprints alternate on right and left sides of the *line of travel.* Hind footprint registers on top of front. As speed increases, hind moves forward of front. Same patterns as a *walk,* but longer *stride.* May be done with body turned to side. See illustration on page xxii.

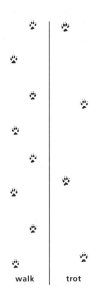

walk   trot

tubercle: rough pinhead-size protuberance on the sole of the foot of a reptile or amphibian.

unguinis: hard material forming nails in humans, hoof walls in deer and their relatives, and claws in other mammals. Composed of hair pasted together by body glues.

walk: a *gait* where evenly spaced footprints alternate on right and left sides of the *line of travel*. Hind footprint registers on top of front. As speed increases, hind moves forward of front. See illustrations on pages xxii and xxvi.

wall: hard material around the edge of each clout of a hoof. Technically the *unguinis,* which also forms human nails and animal claws.

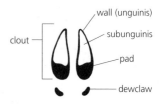

webbing: thin membrane stretched between toes of animals. The webbing may be near the tips of the toes (*distal*), about midway to the toe tips (*mesial*), or attached at the base (*proximal*). A membrane attached to only one toe is called a *fringe*.

width: of a *track,* the greatest distance from the right side of the pads of a foot to the left side, whether the greatest distance is across the toes or palm pads. Measured perpendicular to the *foot axis*. In bird tracks, includes claws if they are attached and indistinguishable from toe pad.

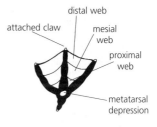

How to use *Scats and Tracks*

Scats and Tracks of the Great Plains is designed for easy use in the field. The gray bars found on the edges of the pages of the track accounts will help you measure scat diameter and footprint size; each of these bars is keyed to the average size of the sign in question. A ruler is provided on the back cover. Below, we provide the background knowledge that every tracker should be familiar with before going to the field or using this book. Please take some time to study this material.

Illustrations

Illustrator Todd Telander applied his great ability to our collections of plaster casts, photographs, and slides, drawing on our experience to produce the most up-to-date and accurate illustrations possible. These drawings—made from the best specimens in a collection of thousands—represent the culmination of decades of tracking experience and are far more accurate than the tracker usually finds in tracking books. The tracks you find on the ground may not have as much detail or be as clear, but it is better to have an excellent drawing to compare to an imperfect track than to have to compare a track to a drawing lacking critical details.

How to use the track accounts

The track accounts in this guide have been grouped by similar footprint characteristics. Each track account represents a single species or a group of species with similar track characteristics. Each account is presented across a two-page spread and is conveniently divided into sections as discussed below.

A brief listing of visual characteristics used to identify

an animal begins each track account, appearing beneath the common and scientific names of the species. These descriptions are general, and great variability of pattern can exist among animals in the field. We recommend consulting appropriate field identification guides.

Track: A concise description of key points of footprints, to be used for identification. The accompanying track illustrations are not at actual size, but, unless otherwise noted, actual (average) length of the footprint is shown as a bar on the right side of the right-hand page. Average width is shown as a bar on the bottom of the right-hand page. In the field, place the appropriate measurement bar next to the track to compare size. To take a numerical measurement, use the ruler printed on the back cover of the book.

The tracks illustrated are all from right feet, except in the entries for birds, where both feet are pictured. Numerical measurements are given in the form *length x width.* Note that measurements of mammal tracks do not include claws, that measurements of bird tracks include claws but do not include toe 1, and that measurements generally do not include parts of the foot that often do not register in a given species's track (e.g., heels in the hind feet of some rodent species).

Trail: The average size of the stride of the most commonly used gait or gaits is given. Other common or characteristic gaits, if any, are discussed. See *track pattern* in the Glossary of Terms on page xxxi. For more information on gaits in tracking, see my *A Field Guide to Mammal Tracking in North America* (1986). Gaits are displayed up the right side of the right-hand page. If the common gait is a walk or trot, however, it may not be illustrated, since all walking and trotting patterns consist of right-left alternating patterns.

Scat: A description of scat supplements the drawing. Average scat width is shown as a bar up the side of the left-hand page. In the field, place the appropriate measurement bar next to the scat to compare sizes. To take a numerical measurement, use the ruler printed on the back cover of the book. Numerical measurements of scat are given under the illustrations in the form *length x width*. In cases of small scat, only width is given; thus, a single measurement always indicates diameter.

Habitat: To aid in locating and differentiating tracks, the animal's habitat preferences are listed. Some animals with large ranges, such as the beaver, are only found in specific habitats.

Similar species: Clues are provided to help differentiate an animal's tracks from similar tracks of other species. With these clues, identification should be possible.

Other sign: Other sign of animals, besides tracks and scat, are listed or illustrated to help with identification, and simply to provide more information on animal lives.

In addition, a distribution map is provided with each account. This gives a generalized picture of where in the Great Plains an animal may be found. Animals may move outside their common range. Animals that require specific habitats will, of course, not be evenly distributed through the shown range.

To make the best use of this guide, carry it with you into the field. When you come across an unfamiliar track or trail, open the book to the appropriate track account and place the page alongside the track for immediate on-site comparison.

Visual key to tracks

This simple key includes birds, reptiles, amphibians, and mammals. It is arranged by the number of toes that show in a good footprint, ranging from no toes to two toes to five toes. Those animals that show four toes in the front print and five toes in the hind are listed between four- and five-toed animals.

Snakes (pp. 20–21)

Series of side-to-side trail undulations.

Deer and Relatives (pp. 134–41)

Two toes form hard, cloven hoof. Dewclaws may show in deep print.

Birds with Webbed Feet (pp. 22–37, 52–53, 64–65)

Three toes facing forward, often a fourth toe facing backward. Claws may be detached from toes. Webbing between two or more toes.

Birds without Webbed Feet (pp. 38–51, 54–63, 66–67)

Three toes facing forward, often a fourth toe facing backward. Claws may be detached from toes.

Wolves, Dogs, and Relatives (pp. 72–79)

Four toes in front and hind prints. Claws usually present and detached. Single anterior lobe on inter-digital pad.

Cougars, Cats, and Relatives (pp. 80–83)

Four toes in front and hind prints. Claws usually absent. Double anterior lobe on interdigital pad.

Rabbits and Relatives (pp. 96–99)

Four toes in front and hind footprint. An exceptionally clear print may show a fifth inner toe in the front footprint. Pads lacking, bottom of foot covered with hair. Long hopping heel in hind print.

Salamanders (pp. 2–3)

Four toes in front print, five toes in hind. Trail wide, often with a tail drag.

Frogs (pp. 6–11)

Four toes in front print, five toes in hind. Long, slender toes. Front print faces center of trail. Distal webbing in hind print.

Toads (pp. 4–5)

Four toes in front print, five toes in hind. Front print faces center of trail. Mesial webbing in hind print. Tubercles may show on front and hind prints.

Rodents (pp. 100–133)

Most have four toes in front prints and five in hind. Beaver has five toes in front print. Front toes show a 1-2-1 grouping, hind show a 1-3-1 grouping. Long hopping heel in hind print.

Lizards (pp. 16–19)

Five toes in front and hind prints. Toes long and slender. Claws may be detached. Tail drag often present in trail.

Turtles (pp. 12–15)

Five toes show in front tracks and four in hind tracks. Front prints toe in and hind prints may toe out. Feet are relatively broad. Claws robust and often visible. Sometimes the claws are the only visible signs on hard ground.

Opossum (pp. 68–69)

Five toes. Distinct hind print with an opposable (like human thumb) inside toe protruding sideways from other toes. Outside toe is slightly separated from middle three toes.

Shrews (pp. 70–71)

Five slender toes present on front and hind feet. In clear prints, four interdigital and two proximal pads may be seen.

Raccoons and Relatives (pp. 84–85)

Five toes in front and hind prints. Toes often round or bulbous at ends. May have long, slender toes.

Weasels and Relatives (pp. 86–95)

Five toes in front and hind prints, though the little toe (on inside of foot) may not show. Toes in a 1-3-1 grouping. Interdigital pad is chevron-shaped. Plantigrade hind foot.

Scats
and
Tracks
of the

Great Plains

Tiger Salamander
Ambystoma tigrinum

Hot dog–size salamander, up to 9.0 inches (23.0 cm) long. Moist, smooth skin. Body brown to black to dark green, with yellow spots or streaks. Tubercles on underside of foot.

Track: Four toes on front foot (often only three show), and five toes on hind foot. The outline of the foot may not show, just toe prints. Even in a clear print, tubercles rarely show.

Trail: Walking stride is about 3.0 inches (7.5 cm). Trail has a wide straddle relative to stride and may show oscillating belly and tail drag marks.

Scat: Soft, pea-size black masses with some hint of oval shape.

scat
0.3 x 0.2 in
0.8 x 0.5 cm

egg mass

SCAT WIDTH

Habitat: Quiet waters around lakes, ponds, and streams in grassland meadow areas and forests.

Similar species: Differs from lizards by wider, oscillating tail drag and by having only four toes on front foot. Larger tracks and trail than newts.

Other sign: Eggs in egg masses are attached individually to underwater plant stems.

front
0.6 x 0.3 in
1.5 x 0.8 cm

hind
0.8 x 0.6 in
2.0 x 1.5 cm

slow walk

FRONT TRACK LENGTH

FRONT TRACK WIDTH

Woodhouse Toad
Bufo woodhousei

Baseball-size toad, up to 5.0 inches (12.5 cm) long. Body is light brown to gray to green, with warty skin and dark spots. A white line runs down the back. Female larger than male.

Track: Four toes on front foot and five on hind. Front feet face in. Tubercles on heel of front foot. Four hind toes face in, while one faces out. Two tubercles may show on the heel of the hind foot and can be confused with toes. Webbing, found only on hind feet, extends at most halfway out to toe tips.

Trail: Walking stride is about 3.0 inches (7.5 cm). Hopping stride generally less than 1.0 foot (0.3 m).

scat
1.0 x 0.3 in
2.5 x 0.8 cm

egg mass

toad imprint in mud

SCAT WIDTH

Scat: Dark brown to black. Long cord, up to five times longer than wide. Sometimes contains insect parts.

Habitat: Lakes, ponds, beaver ponds.

Similar species: Differs from frogs by presence of tubercles on front heels. Hind foot is narrower than frog. Walks and uses short hops more than the usually long-hopping frog.

Other sign: Long strings of egg masses on pond and lake bottoms and floating among vegetation.

walk

front
0.9 x 0.6 in
2.3 x 1.5 cm

hop

mesial web

hind
1.1 x 0.9 in
2.8 x 2.3 cm

FRONT TRACK LENGTH

FRONT TRACK WIDTH

Chorus Frog
Pseudacris triseriata

Silver dollar–size frog less than 1.5 inches (3.8 cm). Highly variable frog with body color from brown to green. Darker stripe pattern varies with subspecies.

Track: Four toes on front foot and five on hind. Front feet face in. Four hind toes face in, with one facing out. Proximal webbing on hind feet extending at most one-quarter of way out to toe tips.

Trail: Hopping stride about 10.0 inches (25.0 cm). Frogs may easily hop 3.0 feet (1.0 m) when in a hurry.

Scat: Black, firm cord with slightly tapering ends.

scat
0.5 x 0.1 in
1.3 x 0.3 cm

egg mass and tadpole

SCAT WIDTH

Habitat: Shallow water with emergent vegetation including pond and lake shores, marshes, and beaver ponds.

Similar species: Lacks the palm tubercles of the front feet of toad. Less webbing between toes. Hops more and longer distances. Smaller than leopard frog.

Other sign: Inconspicuous egg masses consisting of a few eggs in a packet attached to vegetation below waterline.

front
0.6 x 0.4 in
1.5 x 1.0 cm

walk

proximal web

hind
0.8 x 0.6 in
2.0 x 1.5 cm

hop

FRONT TRACK LENGTH

FRONT TRACK WIDTH

Leopard Frog
Rana pipiens

Baseball-size frog, up to
3.5 inches (8.8 cm) long.
Body light to dark brown
or green, with dark spots.
Spots have light borders.
White stripe on jaw.

Track: Four toes on front foot and five on hind. Front feet face in. Four hind toes face in, with one facing out. Webbing, found only on hind feet, is distal, extending most of the way out to toe tips. Toe 1 is thick on male because it serves as the nuptial pad for grasping female during mating.

Trail: Full bound or hopping stride is about 20.0 inches (50.0 cm). May easily hop 3.0 feet (1.0 m) when in a hurry. Occasionally walk.

Scat: Brown to black, with slightly tapered ends.

Habitat: Cold, nonseasonal ponds, streams, and other water sources. May be found in meadows well away from water.

scat
1.5 x 0.4 in
3.8 x 1.0 cm

egg mass

Similar species: Nuptial pad (enlarged pad for holding female during mating) separates male from other hopping amphibians. Differs from toads by more webbing between toes, lack of palm tubercles on front feet, and by hopping more and at longer distances. Larger than chorus frogs.

Other sign: Softball-size egg masses floating just below water surface.

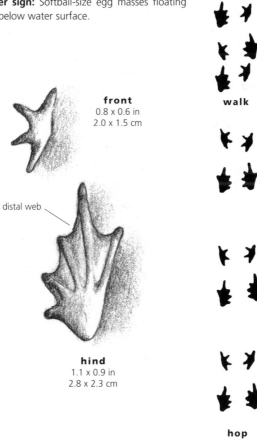

front
0.8 x 0.6 in
2.0 x 1.5 cm

distal web

hind
1.1 x 0.9 in
2.8 x 2.3 cm

walk

hop

FRONT TRACK LENGTH

FRONT TRACK WIDTH

Bullfrog
Rana catesbeiana

Softball-size frog, 4.0 to 8.0 inches (10.0 to 20.0 cm) long. Brownish green to green, becoming light green on head. Legs banded with dark brown to green; small spots on back. Fold of skin around eye and large exposed eardrum.

Track: Four toes on front foot and five on hind. Front feet face in. Three hind toes face in, remaining two face forward or out. Webbing, found only on hind feet, is distal, extending most of the way out to the toe tips. In a clear track, a male's toe 2 (thumb) on front foot appears thicker at base.

Trail: Hopping stride is 24.0 inches (60.0 cm). May easily hop 72.0 inches (180.0 cm).

Scat: Brown to black, with slightly tapered ends.

scat
1.5 x 0.4 in
3.8 x 1.0 cm

SCAT WIDTH

Habitat: Permanent and (usually) quiet water with dense growth of aquatic plants, especially cattails, in plains, woodlands, and forest.

Similar species: Differs from toads by more webbing between toes, lack of palm tubercles on front feet, and by hopping more and at longer distances. Differs from leopard frog and chorus frog by larger feet.

Other sign: Deposits a globular egg mass.

front
1.5 x 1.0 in
3.8 x 2.5 cm

distal web

hind
1.8 x 0.9 in
4.5 x 2.3 cm

walk

hop

FRONT TRACK LENGTH

FRONT TRACK WIDTH

Painted Turtle
Chrysemys picta

A small turtle with
smooth, unkeeled
shells and patterns of
red, yellow, and black.
Length to 8.0 inches
(20.0 cm). Females larger
than males.

Track: Five toes with claws show in front and
back prints. Claws longer on front feet and
those of the male's front feet are two to three
times longer than the female's. Outer toe on
hind foot lacks claw. Distal webbing on front
and hind prints.

Trail: Walking stride averages 4.5 inches (11.3
cm) with a straddle of 4.0 inches (10.0 cm).
Front feet toe in and hind feet toe out. Hind
footprint registers slightly behind. Tail drag
often visible.

Scat: Usually black semiliquid, slightly elongated clumps.

scat
0.9 x 0.2 in
2.3 x 0.5 cm

SCAT WIDTH

Habitat: Ponds, lakes, marshes, swamps, streams, and ditches with abundant vegetation.

Similar species: Differs from snapping turtles by its narrow straight trail.

Other sign: Nests are usually dug in sand in open areas where sun warms eggs.

front
0.8 x 0.7 in without claws
2.0 x 1.8 cm

hind
1.1 x 1.0 in without claws
2.8 x 2.5 cm

walk

FRONT TRACK LENGTH

FRONT TRACK WIDTH

Snapping Turtle
Chelydra serpentina

A large to very large turtle, average weight 10.0 to 30.0 pounds (4.5 to 16.0 kilograms). The robust shell is lined by three toothed ridges. Large head with robust, hooked jaw. Tail longer than half the shell and toothed on top.

Track: Five toes show in front and four in hind tracks. Front prints toe in and hind prints may toe out. Feet are relatively broad. Claws robust and often visible. Sometimes the claws are the only visible sign on hard ground.

Trail: Walking stride ranges from 5.0 to 12.0 inches (12.5 to 30.0 cm). Straddle is wide compared to stride. Tail drag often present.

Scat: Lacks well-defined shape. Color is algae-green to dark black. Often soft.

scat
1.5 in
3.8 cm

SCAT WIDTH

Habitat: Always near water, including swamps, marshes, lakes, streams, and rivers.

Similar species: Broad trail of five-toed, clawed track with a tail drag separates the snapping turtle tracks and trail.

Other sign: Nest in open area where sun warms sand and eggs. Nest may be several inches deep.

front
1.6 x 2.0 in
4.0 x 5.0 cm

hind
3.2 x 2.6 in
8.0 x 6.4 cm

slow walk

FRONT TRACK LENGTH

FRONT TRACK WIDTH

Texas Horned Lizard
Phrynosoma cornutum

Roughly the size of a calling card; body and tail less than 4.0 inches (10.0 cm) long. Body relatively broad, with horns projecting from back of head. Central two head spines are much longer than others. Body mottled gray to brown to tan, closely matching local terrain colors. Two rows of fringe scales along edge of body.

Track: Five relatively long, thin toes on front and hind feet. Hind heel is relatively long. Claws may show.

Trail: Trotting stride is 3.0 inches (7.5 cm). Hind feet mostly register on top of front feet. Relatively wide straddle. Relatively straight tail drag and often a wider body drag.

Scat: Brown pellets three to six times longer than wide; may be tapered. White nitrogenous material may be found on one end.

scat
1.5 x 0.25 in
3.8 x 0.6 cm

Habitat: Determined by presence of fine, loose soil interspersed with firm, sandy or rocky terrain. Found in prairies and open woodlands, from plains high into mountains.

Similar species: Differs from salamanders by having five narrow toes on front feet and relatively straight tail drag. Differs from fence lizard by wider footprint.

Other sign: Scuff marks in loose sand where the lizard buries itself for camouflage.

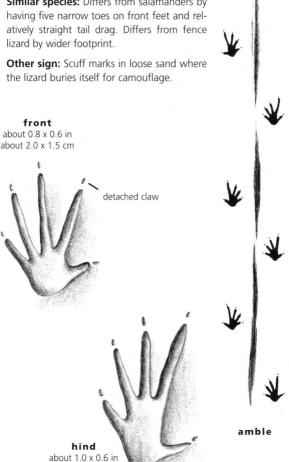

front
about 0.8 x 0.6 in
about 2.0 x 1.5 cm

detached claw

hind
about 1.0 x 0.6 in
about 2.5 x 1.5 cm

amble

FRONT TRACK LENGTH

FRONT TRACK WIDTH

Prairie or Fence Lizard

Sceloporus undulatus

Roughly the size of a
roll of Life Savers; body
about 3.0 inches (7.5 cm),
with dry skin and ridged
scales. Gray to dark brown
above, with black crossbars
(southwestern plains) or longitudinal stripes (southeastern
plains). Considerable subspecies variation.

Track: Five relatively long, thin toes on front
and hind feet. Hind heel is relatively long.
Claws may show.

Trail: Trotting stride is about 3.0 inches (7.5
cm). Hind feet mostly register on top of front
feet. Relatively wide straddle. Straight tail drag.

Scat: Brown cord, six to eight times longer
than wide. White nitrogenous material usually
found on one end.

Habitat: Wide variety of habitats including forests, woodland,
prairie, and rock outcrops. Shelters in bushes, trees, under rocks,
or in logs.

scat
1.5 x 0.25 in
3.8 x 0.6 cm

SCAT WIDTH

Similar species: Differs from salamanders by having five narrow toes on front feet and straighter tail drag. Differs from horned lizard by narrower footprint.

Other sign: Scuff marks in dust may indicate a dust bath.

detached claw

front
0.8 x 0.25 in
2.0 x 0.6 cm

hind
1.0 x 0.3 in
2.5 x 0.8 cm

slow walk

FRONT TRACK LENGTH

FRONT TRACK WIDTH

Snakes
various species

A variety of
snakes, from garter
snakes (*Thamnophis sirtalis*)
to milk snakes (*Lampropeltis*
triangulum) to massasaugas
(*Sistrurus catenatus*) to timber rattlesnakes (*Crotalus*
horridus).

Rattlesnake
Crotalus horridus

Track: No footprint to describe.

Trail: Varies from 1.0 to 4.0 inches (2.5 to 10.0 cm) wide. Characterized by side-to-side undulations of the trail. The period, the distance from one curve to the next, varies by species, age, and speed of the snake. Surface material is usually pushed up at the outside of each curve. Gait is either a side-to-side undulation or sidewinding.

Scat: Black or brown cord, with constrictions and undulations. White nitrogenous material often attached.

scat
4.0 x 0.4 in
10.0 x 1.0 cm

shed skin

SCAT WIDTH

Habitat: Varies widely—from water's edge to rock outcrops to dry sand dunes.

Similar species: Resembles no other track.

Other sign: Shed skin.

lateral undulatory

sidewinding

trail

Common Loon
Gavia immer

Large, long-bodied aquatic bird, average length 24.0 inches (60.0 cm). Dark-colored bird with black-and-white checkered back and neck band. Dark greenish head.

Track: Three toes showing, toes 2 to 4 pointing forward. Toe 1 does not register. Toes 2, 3, and 4 have claws and distal webbing.

Trail: Walking stride is 10.0 inches (25.0 cm) with a 7.0-inch (18.0-cm) straddle. Toes turn inward. Foot drag marks usually evident because the loon's legs are placed far back on its body making walking difficult and causing the loon to drag its feet.

Scat: Not known.

nest

Habitat: Freshwater lakes and rivers; near shore on ocean.

Similar species: Differs from all other aquatic birds by heavy drag marks in trail and relatively long, narrow feet.

Other sign: Large nest on reeds and brush at edge of water. Eggs appear large in small nest.

distal web

feet
5.25 x 4.3 in
13.1 x 10.8 cm

walk

TRACK LENGTH

TRACK WIDTH (50%)

White Pelican
Pelecanus erythrorhynchos

Large aquatic bird, average length more than 60.0 inches (150.0 cm), with a wingspan of more than 8.0 feet (2.4 m). White with black primary wing feathers. Large bill is yellow to orange.

Track: Four long, slender toes. Toe 1 offset to side of track. Feet *totipalmate*, with webbing between all four toes. Webbing distal and slightly convex between toes. Claws attached.

Trail: Walking stride averages 16.0 inches (40.0 cm). Toes turn inward.

Scat: Shapeless, brownish-white mass.

Habitat: Lakes, marshes, and bays. During summer, found in freshwater lakes; in winter, found in salt water.

ground nest

Similar species: Differs from all other web-footed birds except cormorant by being toti-palmate. Differs from cormorant by having attached claws.

Other sign: Nests on ground in large island colonies.

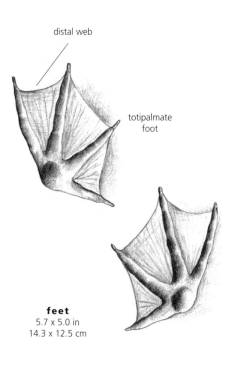

distal web

totipalmate foot

feet
5.7 x 5.0 in
14.3 x 12.5 cm

walk

TRACK LENGTH

TRACK WIDTH (50%)

Double-crested Cormorant
Phalacrocorax auritus

Large aquatic bird, average length
more than 32.0 inches (80.0 cm),
with a wingspan of more than
4.3 feet (1.3 cm). Dark-colored
body with orange throat
patch. Crest of two white
feathers behind eye, which
may be difficult to see.

Track: Four long, slender
toes. Toe 1 offset to side of track. Toe 4 is
longest. Feet *totipalmate,* i.e., with webbing
between all four toes. Webbing distal and
slightly convex between toes. Claws detached.

Trail: Walking stride is about 10.0 inches (25.0
cm). Walks awkwardly on land, with a short
stride for its size. Toes turn inward.

Scat: Shapeless, nearly liquid white mass.

ground nest

Habitat: Saltwater islands, bays, and cliffs. Freshwater lakes, ponds, and swamps.

Similar species: Differs from all other web-footed birds except pelican by being totipalmate. Differs from pelican by having detached claws.

Other sign: Nests in colonies on ground or in trees. Acidic scat kills trees and ground vegetation.

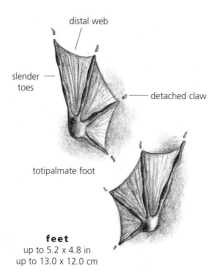

distal web

slender — toes

detached claw

totipalmate foot

feet
up to 5.2 x 4.8 in
up to 13.0 x 12.0 cm

walk

TRACK LENGTH

TRACK WIDTH (50%)

Green-backed Heron
Butorides striatus

Medium-size wading bird, average length 14.0 inches (35.0 cm). Male and female similar in overall appearance: blue to greenish body, with reddish brown neck and yellowish legs.

Track: Four toes, toes 2 to 4 pointing forward. Small proximal web between toes 3 and 4. Footprint is asymmetrical, with toe 1 set to inside of foot axis (drawn through toe 3). On hard ground, metatarsal pad may not show (that is, toes may appear unconnected).

Trail: Walking stride about 10.0 inches (25.0 cm). Trail is fairly straight and feet point forward.

Scat: Semiliquid, predominantly white. Solid cords of scat vary from 1.0 to 3.0 inches (2.5 to 7.5 cm) and may contain fish, insects, frogs, and salamanders.

cough pellet

12.0 in

nest
4 to 5 eggs common

Habitat: Fresh- and saltwater areas along ponds, streams, lakes, swamps, and beaches where heavily wooded.

Similar species: Smaller version of great blue heron track (6.5 in/16.5 cm). Differs from other shore-edge tracks by asymmetrical placement of toes.

Other sign: Undigested material may be coughed up as pellets.

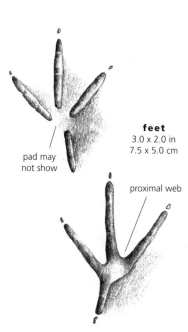

pad may not show

feet
3.0 x 2.0 in
7.5 x 5.0 cm

proximal web

walk

TRACK LENGTH

TRACK WIDTH

Great Blue Heron
Ardea herodias

Large wading bird, average length
45.0 inches (113.0 cm). Male and
female similar in overall appearance: gray-blue body, with white
neck and yellow beak. Black crown
extends on feathers off rear of head.

Track: Four toes, toes 2 to 4 pointing
forward. Small proximal web between
toes 3 and 4. Footprint is asymmetrical,
with toe 1 set to inside of foot axis
(drawn through toe 3). Toe 1 is about 1.5
inches (3.8 cm); toe 2 is longer than 1, though
shorter than 3 and 4. On hard ground,
metatarsal pad may not show (that is, toes may
appear unconnected).

Trail: Walking stride about 20.0 inches (50.0
cm). Trail is fairly straight and feet point forward.

Scat: Semiliquid, predominantly white. Solid
cords of scat vary from 2.0 to 3.0 inches (5.0 to 7.5 cm) in length,

cough pellet

nest

rookery

and may contain fish, frogs, salamanders, and even small rodents. Ground beneath nests becomes coated with droppings.

Habitat: Frequents backwater eddies along riverbanks and shallow edges of lakes.

Similar species: Differs from other shore-edge tracks by large size and asymmetrical placement of toes.

Other sign: Large colonies of nests high in trees. Undigested material may be coughed up as pellets.

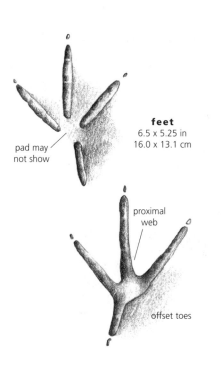

feet
6.5 x 5.25 in
16.0 x 13.1 cm

pad may
not show

proximal
web

offset toes

walk

Trumpeter Swan
Cygnus buccinator

Large aquatic bird, length averaging 60.0 inches (150.0 cm). Male larger than female. Adult is all white, with a black beak. Immature swan has gray plumage. Male and female identically colored.

Track: Four toes. Toes 2 to 4, which point forward, usually register. Toe 1 points rearward and only occasionally shows. Distal webbing between toes 2, 3, and 4. Toes 2 and 4 tend to converge slightly near tips. Claws are broad, blunt, and attached to toes. Feet turned in.

Trail: Walking stride is about 14.0 inches (35.0 cm).

Scat: Cord, five to eight times longer than wide. Often greenish and coated with white nitrogenous deposits.

scat
3.5 x 0.5 in
8.8 x 1.3 cm

SCAT WIDTH

Habitat: Ponds, lakes, slowly flowing streams and rivers.

Similar species: Larger than ducks and geese. Differs from pelican and cormorant by lacking webbing between toes 1 and 2. Larger than gulls, also differing from them by having convergent toes and distal webbing.

Other sign: Nests on elevated areas such as beaver lodges and muskrat houses, or on the ground. Eggs larger than eggs of Canada goose.

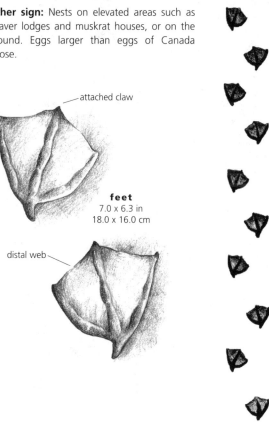

attached claw

feet
7.0 x 6.3 in
18.0 x 16.0 cm

distal web

walk

TRACK LENGTH (50%)

TRACK WIDTH (50%)

Mallard
Anas platyrhynchos

Aquatic birds with webbed feet, varying in size from the small bufflehead through mallards (*Anas platyrhynchos*) to pintails. Length ranges from 14.0 to 24.0 inches (35.0 to 60.0 cm). Large variety in body patterns among species. Males generally more brightly colored than females.

Track: Four toes. Toes 2 to 4, which point forward, usually register. Toe 1 points rearward and may not show. Distal webbing between toes 2, 3, and 4. Webbing concave between toes. Toes 2 and 4 tend to converge near tips. Claws are broad, blunt, and attached to toes. Feet turned in.

Trail: Walking stride of a mallard (illustrated here) is about 4.0 inches (10.0 cm).

scat
2.0 x 0.25 in
5.0 x 0.6 cm

SCAT WIDTH

Scat: Pencil-size cords, four to eight times longer than wide. Often greenish and coated with white nitrogenous deposits.

Habitat: Ponds, lakes, marshes, streams, rivers, and bays.

Similar species: Tracks differ from geese and swan by smaller size. Differ from pelicans and cormorants by lacking webbing between toes 1 and 2. Differ from gulls by having convergent toes.

Other sign: Nests may be on the ground, in tree cavities, or on floating mats. Eggs roughly the size of chicken eggs, though there may be great variation among species.

distal web

feet
2.2 x 2.4 in
5.5 x 6.0 cm

convergent toes

walk

TRACK LENGTH

TRACK WIDTH

Canada Goose
Branta canadensis

Medium-size
aquatic bird, average
length 30.0 inches (75.0
cm). Considerable size
variation among sub-
species. Black head and
neck, with a white chin
band. Back is olive
brown. Male and female
similarly colored.

Track: Four toes. Toes 2 to 4, which point forward, usually register. Toe 1 points rearward
and only occasionally shows. Distal webbing
between toes 2, 3, and 4. Toes 2 and 4 tend to
converge slightly near tips. Claws are broad,
blunt, and usually attached to toes. Feet turn in.

Trail: Walking stride is about 12.0 inches (30.0
cm).

scat
3.0 x 0.4 in
7.5 x 1.0 cm

SCAT WIDTH

Scat: Cord, five to eight times longer than wide. As long as 3.5 inches (8.8 cm). Often greenish and coated with white nitrogenous deposits.

Habitat: Ponds, lakes, marshes, streams, rivers, and bays.

Similar species: Larger than most ducks and smaller than swans. Differs from pelican and cormorant by lacking webbing between toes 1 and 2. Larger than gulls, and differing from them by having convergent toes and distal webbing.

Other sign: Nests on ground, sometimes on cliff ledges, and in abandoned heron and raptor nests. Eggs larger than chicken eggs.

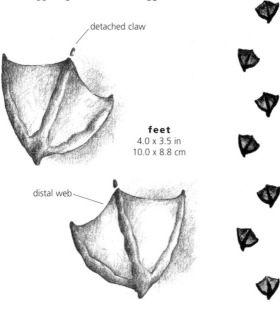

detached claw

feet
4.0 x 3.5 in
10.0 x 8.8 cm

distal web

walk

TRACK LENGTH

TRACK WIDTH

Red-tailed Hawk
Buteo jamaicenisis

Medium-size birds, up to 25.0 inches (63.0 cm) in length, with wingspans of 50.0 inches (125.0 cm). The red-tailed hawk (*Buteo jamaicensis*) is a highly variable, dark-colored hawk with red tail feathers. Light phase has a dark belly band.

Track: Four wide, robust toes. Toes 2 to 4 point forward. Claws are long, sharp, and not attached to the toe print.

Trail: Walking stride of a red-tailed hawk (illustrated here) is about 12.0 inches (30.0 cm). Hops or runs after prey on the ground. Claws may drag in soft mud, creating a fringe along sides of footprint.

Scat: Semiliquid, primarily white with some brown intermixed. Unlike owls, scat is ejected with force, sometimes leaving a trail. Whitish piles and vertical streaks below nests.

cough pellets

Habitat: Woodland and open country with scattered trees.

Similar species: Smaller than eagles. Differ from owls by having three toes pointing forward. Differ from geese and swans by lacking webbing. Differ from herons and cranes by having symmetrical feet.

Other sign: Cough pellets may be 1.5 to 4.0 inches (3.8 to 10.0 cm) long.

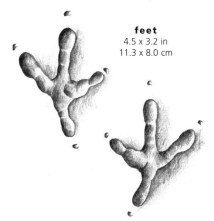

feet
4.5 x 3.2 in
11.3 x 8.0 cm

walk

Eagles
two species

Large birds, averaging
35.0 inches (88.0 cm) in
length, with wingspans
of 80.0 inches (200.0
cm). Brown bodies.
Adult golden eagle
(*Aquila chrysaetos*) has
golden feathers over head and
neck. Adult bald eagle (*Haliaeetus leucocephalus*) has white head, neck, and tail feathers.

Bald eagle
Haliaeetus leucocephalus

Track: Four wide, robust toes. Toes 2 to 4 point forward. Lacks webbing and metatarsal pad. Claws are long, sharp, and not attached to the toe print.

Trail: Walking stride about 18.0 inches (45.0 cm). Golden eagle will run after prey on the ground.

Scat: Semiliquid, primarily white with some brown intermixed.

Habitat: Golden eagle found in hilly areas and hunts over open country. Bald eagle usually found near lakes and rivers.

cough pellet

urine stain on rock

Similar species: Larger than hawk's track, which is less than 3.0 inches (7.5 cm). Differ from owls by having three toes pointing forward. Differ from geese and swans by lacking webbing. Differ from herons and cranes by having symmetrical feet.

Other sign: Cough pellets may be 5.0 x 1.5 inches (12.5 x 3.8 cm). Nests may be 6.0 feet (2.0 m) in diameter.

broad toe

detached claw

feet
6.0 x 4.5 in
15.0 x 11.3 cm

heel lacking

walk

TRACK LENGTH

TRACK WIDTH (50%)

Ring-necked Pheasant
Phasianus colchicus

A large, chickenlike bird, males 33.0 inches (84.0 cm) and females 21.0 inches (53.0 cm) in length. Male brightly colored with green head, mottled brown, black, bronze, and white body. Female is a mottled buffy brown. Male has a long, pointed tail.

Track: Four toes, with toes 2 to 4 pointing forward. Toe 1, relatively short, may not show. Toes are relatively wide and lack webbing. Feet point forward to slightly inward.

Trail: Walking stride is about 11.0 inches (28.0 cm). Narrow trail; toes neither toe in or out.

scat
0.8 x 0.4 in
2.0 x 1.0 cm

SCAT WIDTH

Scat: Variable bulbous dropping, greenish brown with white ends. Sometimes two or more pieces sticking together.

Habitat: Bushy country, woodland edges, farmlands, and wind rows.

Similar species: Differ from grouse by longer stride and narrower straddle. Smaller tracks differentiate from turkey.

Other sign: Nest in grass is a shallow depression occasionally lined with some grass.

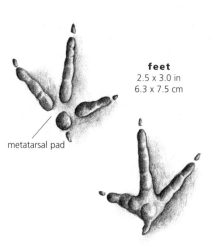

feet
2.5 x 3.0 in
6.3 x 7.5 cm

metatarsal pad

walk

TRACK LENGTH

TRACK WIDTH

Turkey

Meleagris gallopavo

Large, ground-dwelling bird. Males average 45.0 inches (113.0 cm) and females 35.0 inches (88.0 cm) in length. Smaller and more slender than the domesticated Thanksgiving turkey. Male has a dark-brown to black body, with white stripes on flight feather; tail feathers are tipped with brownish white. Color of female's feathers is similar but dull. Male also has red *wattles*, folds of skin hanging from the chin.

Track: Four broad, robust toes. Toes 2 to 4 face forward. Hind toe (toe 1) only occasionally registers, and then in a straight line with toe 4. Only the claw or tip of toe 1 registers. Metatarsal pad present, though it may be unattached to toes. Claws narrow and usually attached to toe.

Trail: Walking stride 15.0 inches (38.0 cm). Foot axis may vary, pointing into the line of travel or turning slightly out.

scat
3.0 x 0.5 in
7.5 x 1.3 cm

tracks with scratch marks

SCAT WIDTH

Scat: Solid scat is long, up to 3.0 inches (7.5 cm), narrow, and brown with greenish-white nitrogenous material on ends. Also produces a soft scat that piles in a shapeless mass on ground.

Habitat: Open forest, shrubland, and wooded swamps, in trees with lateral branches for roosting at night.

Similar species: Differs from other birds by wide, robust toes. Tracks larger than other ground-dwelling birds. Lacks webbing of ducks and certain other aquatic birds. Separated from eagles by presence (usually) of metatarsal pad. Toes 2 and 4 point forward to a greater degree than those of crane.

Other sign: Scratches on ground where turkey digs for seeds, acorns, nuts, and insects.

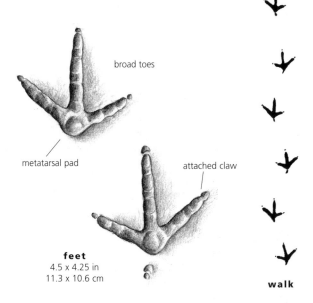

broad toes

metatarsal pad

attached claw

feet
4.5 x 4.25 in
11.3 x 10.6 cm

walk

TRACK LENGTH

TRACK WIDTH (50%)

Bobwhite
Colinus virginianus

Size comparable to a small chicken, 9.0 inches (23.0 cm) in length. Mottled reddish brown with a short gray-colored tail. Male with white stripes on face and throat, brownish in female.

Track: Four toes, with toes 2 to 4 pointing forward. Toe 1, relatively short, may be detached or not show. Toes are relatively wide and lack webbing. Feet point forward to slightly inward.

Trail: Walking stride is about 6.0 inches (15.0 cm). Trail is straight but feet toe in.

Scat: Light to dark brown, sometimes with white nitrogenous covering.

depressions in dust from chicks

scat
1.4 x 0.2 in
3.5 x 0.5 cm

SCAT WIDTH

Habitat: Tall grasslands, brushlands, open woodlands, and cultivated fields.

Similar species: Tracks smaller than grouse. Differ from other forest birds by wide, robust toe size and short toe 1. Bobwhite trails can be differentiated from those of other forest birds by their short strides and wide straddles.

Other sign: Ground roost is a circle of shallow body depressions where birds sleep with their heads pointing out. Nest is a shallow depression under "woven" grass with a side entrance.

walk

feet
1.75 x 1.5 in
4.4 x 3.8 cm

TRACK LENGTH

TRACK WIDTH

Coot

Fulica americana

Medium-size aquatic bird, average length 15.0 inches (38.0 cm). Slate-black body, with white beak extending into small brown forehead shield.

Track: Four toes showing, toes 2 to 4 pointing forward. Toe 1 angles inward. Toes 2, 3, and 4 have fringe of webbing with indented lobes. Long, pointed claws, especially those on toe 1, may be separated from toes.

Trail: Walking stride 10.0 inches (25.0 cm); tends to wander when walking. Foot axis parallel to line of travel.

Scat: White liquid.

Habitat: Freshwater lakes and ponds having shallow water where reeds and rushes grow.

Similar species: Differs from all other aquatic birds by the indented lobes on each toe.

Other sign: Floating nest built from cattails, sedges, and rushes, rising several inches above the water.

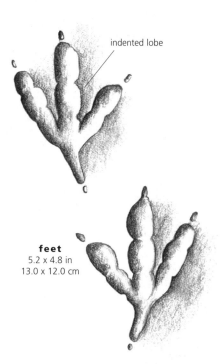

indented lobe

feet
5.2 x 4.8 in
13.0 x 12.0 cm

walk

TRACK LENGTH

TRACK WIDTH (50%)

Sandhill Crane
Grus canadensis

Large bird, average length 39.0 inches (98.0 cm). Appearance of males and females similar: grayish, with red crown on head, and white cheeks and chin. Summers in the north and winters in the south (dark shade on map), but may be found (light shade) occasionally nesting their young.

Track: Four toes, toes 2 to 4 showing. Outside toes opposed by nearly 180 degrees. Toe 3 is longer than 2 and 4. Small proximal web between toes 2 and 3 rarely shows. Claws usually attached to toes, though claw of toe 1 rarely shows. Feet point forward.

Trail: Walking stride about 24.0 inches (60.0 cm). Often runs, extending its stride. Tracks have a narrow straddle, being nearly in line with one another.

Scat: Similar to, but smaller than, Canada goose. Brown in color, with some vegetation. Can contain bones of small mammals, reptiles, and amphibians.

scat
2.5 x 0.3 in
6.3 x 0.8 cm

SCAT WIDTH

Habitat: Meadows, marshes, grasslands, and fields.

Similar species: Differs from ducks, geese, swans, and herons by having only small proximal web. Differs from large raptors by lacking toe 1.

Other sign: Listen for its rattling call, which suggests to some what dinosaurs may have sounded like.

attached claw

detached claw

feet
4.0 x 5.2 in
10.0 x 13.0 cm

walk

TRACK LENGTH

TRACK WIDTH (50%)

Shorebirds
various species

Many birds, such as avocets
(*Recurvirostra ameri-
cana*) illustrated here,
sandpipers, killdeer, curlews,
and snipes. Length varies from
6.0 to 18.0 inches (15.0 to 45.0 cm).
All have similar footprints and
differentiation is difficult.

Track: For avocets (illustrated here) four narrow toes, although toe 1 may not show. Toes 2 to 4 face forward and are nearly symmetrical around toe 3. Outer toe angle often greater than 120 degrees. Small, proximal webbing between toes 2, 3, and 4 may be visible, though curlews and sandpipers have proximal webbing only between toes 3 and 4. Avocets exhibit mesial webbing.

Trail: Shorebirds are constantly running along the water's edge. Stride varies from 4.0 to 20.0 inches (10.0 to 50.0 cm).

Scat: Small and semiliquid. Brown, green, and white mixed.

Habitat: Water's edge at lakes, rivers, streams, bays, and wastewater treatment plants.

**nest in grass
with twigs**

Similar species: Differ from song- or perching birds by the weak showing of toe 1, which in perching birds is strong and used to grasp branches. Outer toe angle of songbirds is less than 90 degrees. Shorebirds walk or run, but most songbirds hop.

Other sign: Myriad roundish holes where beak pushed into the sand in pursuit of insects.

feet
2.4 x 2.9 in
6.0 x 7.3 cm

may not show

walk

TRACK LENGTH

TRACK WIDTH

Owls
various species

Considerable variation in length, from the saw-whet owl (*Aegolius acadicus*), 8.0 inches (20.0 cm), to the short-eared owl (*Asio flammeus*) illustrated here, 15.0 inches (38.0 cm), to the great horned owl (*Bubo virginianus*), 25.0 inches (63.0 cm). All species have immobile eyes offset by facial disks of feathers. Great variability in appearance between species. Typical body colors are grays, browns, and reddish browns.

Track: Four broad toes, with two paired and facing forward. Toe 4 position is not fixed and may face back or out. Lack webbing and metatarsal pads. Claws long and detached from footprint. Tracks of short-eared owl illustrated here.

Trail: Walking stride varies considerably among species, from 3.0 to 10.0 inches (7.5 to 25.0 cm).

cough pellet

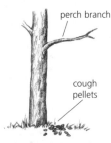

perch branch

cough pellets

perch with pellets

Scat: Semiliquid, primarily white.

Habitat: Forested areas. Some species, such as barn owls, will readily use human structures.

Similar species: Differ from most birds in toes 2 and 3 being paired, nearly parallel, and pointing forward. Differ from woodpeckers by toes being wide and robust, and by toes 1 and 4 being much shorter than toes 2 and 3.

Other sign: Cough pellets below a roost. Diameter of cough pellets ranges from 0.25 to 1.0 inch (0.6 to 2.5 cm) and is directly related to the size of the owl. Pellets are shiny and black when new but turn gray with age.

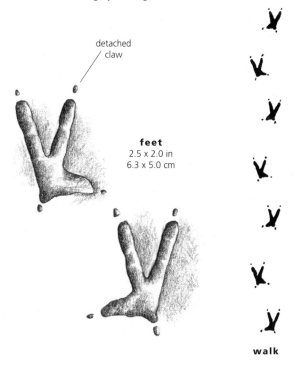

detached claw

feet
2.5 x 2.0 in
6.3 x 5.0 cm

walk

Woodpeckers
various species

Considerable variation in size. The flicker (*Colaptes auratus*) is a medium-size woodpecker, slightly larger than the American robin, average length 12.0 inches (30.0 cm). Male has brown-barred back, black chest, white rump, and red or black whisker stripe, and is yellow under wings. Female lacks whisker stripe.

Track: Four toes, with two parallel and pointing forward. Toes 1 and 4 point backward and are not equal in length. Strong, rigid tail feathers may show on ground.

Trail: Walking stride of the flicker (illustrated here) is about 3.0 inches (7.5 cm). Hopping stride is about 4.0 inches (10.0 cm).

Scat: Cord, about four or more times longer than wide. Often contains undigested parts of insects.

Habitat: Open woodlands, dense forests, and around towns.

Similar species: Differs from three-toed woodpecker by presence of toe 1. Differs from other birds its size by having two toes pointing forward.

scat
1.0 x 0.25 in
2.5 x 0.6 cm

SCAT WIDTH

Other sign: Excavates and nests in tree cavities. Does not add bedding material to cavity nest.

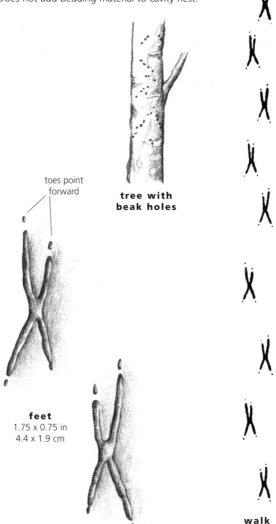

toes point forward

tree with beak holes

feet
1.75 x 0.75 in
4.4 x 1.9 cm

walk

TRACK LENGTH

TRACK WIDTH

Blue Jay
Cyanocitta cristata

Small bird with blue
body and white
markings on wings.
Prominent blue crest
and black throat band.
Average length about
11.0 inches (28.0 cm).

Track: Narrow track with four narrow toes,
toes 2 to 4 facing forward and not widely
splayed. Toe 1 as long as toes 2, 3, and 4.
Toe 1 broader than other toes. Lacks webbing and metatarsal pad. Claws long, especially on toe 1.

Trail: Hopping stride is 4.0 to 5.0 inches
(10.0 to 12.5 cm). Occasionally walks.

Scat: Semiliquid, brown to black with white
intermixed.

Habitat: Woodlands, gardens, and parks.

Similar species: Differs from songbirds by larger size and relatively narrow footprint. Smaller and narrower than crows and ravens.

Other sign: Nest, on horizontal branch or tree crotch, is compact and occasionally cemented with mud.

hop

feet
2.2 x 0.5 in
5.5 x 1.3 cm

walk

TRACK LENGTH

TRACK WIDTH

Crow
Corvus brachyrhynchos

Medium-size (17.0 in/43.0 cm) black bird with strong beak (smaller than raven's). Sides of tail are parallel in flight, not wedge shaped. Black feet and legs.

Track: Four toes, three facing forward. Toe 1 nearly equals toes 2, 3, and 4. Lacks webbing. Metatarsal pad present. Claws long and often detached from footprint. The footprint length of 2.5 inches (6.3 cm) includes toe 4, which adds 0.7 inch (1.8 cm).

Trail: Walking stride varies but is about 5.0 inches (12.5 cm). Crows both walk and hop and may run with a long stride.

Scat: Semiliquid brown and white, but may contain remnants of food from their omnivorous diet.

Habitat: Roadside, woodlands, farms, orchards, and lake and ocean shores.

cough pellet

Similar species: Raven track and trail is much larger than crow's. Lack the paired forward facing toes of owls. Lack long toe 1 of hawks.

Other sign: Cough pellets up to 1.0 x 0.4 inches (2.5 x 1.0 cm). Pellets may contain berries, seeds, nuts, insect parts, and snails, among other items of its varied diet.

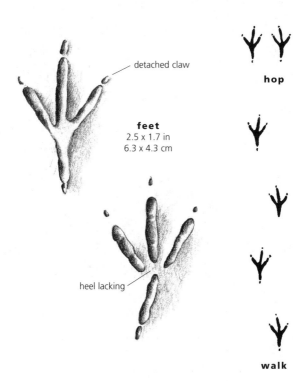

detached claw

feet
2.5 x 1.7 in
6.3 x 4.3 cm

heel lacking

hop

walk

TRACK LENGTH

TRACK WIDTH

Black-billed Magpie
Pica pica

Black and iridescent
green body, wings, and
unusually long tail.
Average length about
20.0 inches (50.0 cm).
Belly is white. Beak is
black.

Track: Four medium-wide toes, three facing forward. Toe 1 nearly as long as toes 2, 3, and 4. Lacks webbing and metatarsal pad. Claws long and detached from footprint.

Trail: Walking stride is about 6.0 inches (15.0 cm).

Scat: Semiliquid, brown with white inter-mixed.

cough pellet

Habitat: Lower mountains, in open woodlands, thickets, along stream edges. Often found near human habitation.

Similar species: Differs from songbirds by larger size and relatively wide toes. Smaller than crows and ravens.

Other sign: Caches food in trees and under bark. Cough pellets are 1.25 x 0.4 inches (3.1 x 1.0 cm).

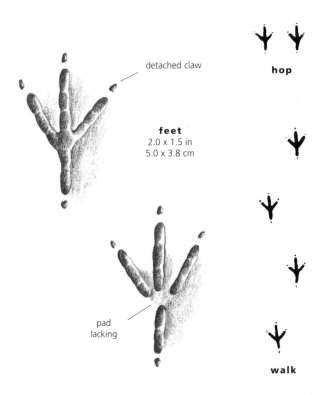

detached claw

feet
2.0 x 1.5 in
5.0 x 3.8 cm

hop

pad lacking

walk

TRACK LENGTH

TRACK WIDTH

Spotted Sandpiper
Actitis macularia

Type of shorebird, along with killdeer, curlews, and snipes. Average length varies from 6.0 to 18.0 inches (15.0 to 45.0 cm). All have similar footprints and differentiation is difficult.

Track: Four narrow toes, although toe 1 may not show. Toes 2 to 4 face forward and are nearly symmetrical around toe 3. Outer toe angle often greater than 120 degrees. Small, proximal webbing between toes 2, 3, and 4 may be visible, though curlews and sandpipers have proximal webbing only between toes 3 and 4.

Trail: Shorebirds are constantly running along the water's edge. Stride varies from 4.0 to 20.0 inches (10.0 to 50.0 cm).

Scat: Small and semiliquid. Browns, green and white mixed.

beach with beak holes

Habitat: Water's edge at lakes, rivers, streams, wastewater treatment plants.

Similar species: Differ from song- or perching birds by the weak showing of toe 1, which in perching birds is strong and used to grasp branches. Outer toe angle of songbirds is less than 90 degrees. Shorebirds walk, but most songbirds hop.

Other sign: Myriad roundish holes where beak pushed into the sand in pursuit of insects.

feet
1.25 x 1.0 in
3.1 x 2.5 cm

Roadrunner
Geococcyx californianus

Medium-size, ground-dwelling cuckoo, averaging 23.0 inches (58.0 cm), who runs rapidly and seldom flies. Brown and white-streaked body with a dark crest. Long tail, tipped with white.

Track: Four relatively long, slender toes. Toes 1 and 4 point backward. Toes 1 and 4 similar in length to toes 2 and 3. Claws on toes 2 and 3 detached and prominent. Claws on toes 1 and 4 usually do not register.

Trail: Running stride averages 16.0 inches (40.0 cm), but may be considerably longer as the roadrunner can leave the ground in mid-stride.

Scat: No record.

Habitat: Shrub desert including mesquite and chaparral.

Similar species: Four toes, with two pointing forward includes ospreys, owls, cuckoos, kingfishers, and four-toed woodpeckers. Woodpecker track distinct in that toes 1 and 4 are not similar in length to toes 2 and 3. Toes 2 and 3 of the king-fisher are closely joined by webbing. Osprey and owl tracks have broader, more robust toes. Habitat is a good clue to identification.

Other sign: Nest in low thicket or cactus may contain snake skins and mammal feces.

feet
2.4 x 1.4 in
6.0 x 3.5 cm

walk

TRACK LENGTH

TRACK WIDTH

Opossum
Didelphis marsupialis

The size of a large domestic cat, but more stout, nearly hairless, and with a round, ratlike tail. Weight varies from 8.0 to 14.0 pounds (3.5 to 6.5 kg). Face whitish, with thin, black-edged ears. Body is whitish with gray and black hairs interspersed.

Track: Five toes. Hind print is distinctive, with an opposable (like the human thumb) inside toe protruding sideways from other toes. Outside toe is slightly separated from middle three toes. Front footprint is wider than long and shows long toes that widen slightly toward the end.

Trail: Walking stride 18.0 inches (45.0 cm). Walking trail often reflects slow movement, with hind footprint registering behind the front. Trail is sloppy and footprints seldom register directly. Tail drag often shows. Walking pattern occasionally similar to that of the raccoon, where the hind footprint registers beside the front footprint.

scat shape is highly variable

scat
4.0 x 0.5 in
10.0 x 1.3 cm

Scat: Highly variable shape and size and lack of distinctive form reflect highly variable, omnivorous diet. Single scat may be up to 4.0 inches (10.0 cm) long.

Habitat: Prefers riparian areas, woodlands, and farmyards. Habitat is not restricted by diet, as the opossum will eat small mammals, birds, eggs, reptiles, amphibians, fish, carrion, fruit, and any garbage it can find.

Similar species: Trail may be confused with those of muskrats, woodrats, and domestic rats when a tail drag is present. However, the distinctive hind footprint and large size of the opossum footprint identify its trail.

Other sign: Dens in logs, stumps, rock crevices, and dens of other animals.

amble

walk

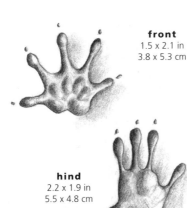

front
1.5 x 2.1 in
3.8 x 5.3 cm

hind
2.2 x 1.9 in
5.5 x 4.8 cm

opposable toe

FRONT TRACK LENGTH

FRONT TRACK WIDTH

Shrews
various species

Masked shrew
Sorex cinereus

Smaller than mice, less
than 0.25 ounce (7.0 g).
Long, pointed nose.
Minute eyes and ears.
Color brown to black, with
gray to white belly. Eat mostly
insects. The masked shrew (*Sorex
cinereus*) is illustrated here.

Track: Five slender toes are present on front
and hind feet. In clear prints, four interdigital
and two proximal pads may be seen.

Trail: Hopping stride seldom more than 2.0
inches (5.0 cm). The group of tracks is less than
1.0 inch (2.5 cm) long. Seldom is the stride
more than three times the group.

Scat: Usually small pellets with tapered ends.

Habitat: Found everywhere from grasslands to
alpine areas. Look for tracks in wet, fine mud
of riparian areas or in snow along logs or the edges of buildings.
Wood piles and leaf litter make good homes.

——— tapered ends

scat
0.2 x 0.1 in
0.5 x 0.3 cm

insect remains

Similar species: Differ from mice and voles by having five toes on front foot.

Other sign: After eating, leave body parts from insects they have killed. Often burrow just below the surface of the snow, opening tunnels that partially collapse and expose their route. Trails in the snow radiate from holes like spokes of a wheel.

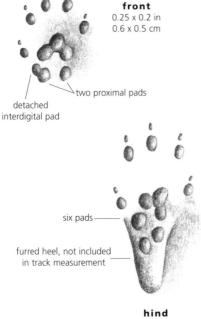

front
0.25 x 0.2 in
0.6 x 0.5 cm

two proximal pads

detached
interdigital pad

six pads

furred heel, not included
in track measurement

hind
0.3 x 0.2 in
0.8 x 0.5 cm

bound

FRONT TRACK LENGTH

FRONT TRACK WIDTH

Red Fox
Vulpes vulpes

Border collie–size, 6.0 to 15.0 pounds (3.0 to 7.0 kg). Reddish yellow, with black stockings and a white tip on the tail. Regional color phases include silver, black, cross, and bluish gray. Long, pointed ears and elongate, pointed muzzle.

Track: Claws prominent. One lobe on the leading edge of the interdigital pad. Inside toe slightly larger than outside. A ridge of callus present across interdigital pad, but difficult to detect on hind footprint. Front foot larger than hind.

Trail: Trotting stride averages 32.0 inches (80.0 cm). Typically uses a trotting gait and, occasionally, a 2 x 2 trot with body turned to the side. Walks more than coyote, especially in shrubs.

Scat: Often has tapered tail. Composition varies. Mouse or rabbit fur, berries, and insects are common. Bird feathers and plant remains often present.

scat
2.0 x 0.6 in
5.0 x 1.5 cm

log

SCAT WIDTH

Habitat: Found in a variety of habitats from brush to croplands to mixed hard- and softwood forest. Prefers edges, where hunting for small mammals is good. Also found in urban areas, where cover is available during the daytime. Not found in dense forests.

Similar species: Differs from other canids by having a ridge of callus on the interdigital pad. Track tends to be larger than that of gray fox, and usually shows claws. Differs from bobcat in having only one lobe on the interdigital pad and claws (usually) showing.

Other sign: Multiple dens are used each season. Often digs own den. A given den may be used for several years. Look for small bones around den entrance. Scat has a diagnostic musky odor, produced by a musk gland on the top of the tail. Learn to identify this unique foxy odor. Foxes tightrope-walk on narrow logs. May take over woodchuck dens.

side trot

trot

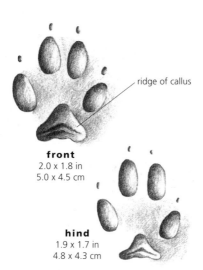

ridge of callus

front
2.0 x 1.8 in
5.0 x 4.5 cm

hind
1.9 x 1.7 in
4.8 x 4.3 cm

FRONT TRACK LENGTH

FRONT TRACK WIDTH

Gray Fox
Urocyon cinereoargenteus

Smaller than a border collie, 8.0 to 11.0 pounds (4.0 to 5.0 kg). Body color is pepper-and-salt. A black stripe runs down the back and upper side of tail. Sides are reddish. Tip of tail is black. Long, pointed ears and elongate, pointed muzzle.

Track: Small for a canid, somewhat broad and therefore somewhat catlike. Claws, rarely present in track, are very small and sharp, giving the gray fox the ability to climb trees like a cat. Front foot larger than hind.

Trail: Generally a trot. Trotting stride averages 24.0 inches (60.0 cm). Walks more than coyote.

Scat: Often has tapered tail. Composition varies, as the gray fox is opportunistic when feeding. Rabbit fur is most common, followed by fur of other small mammals, berries, and insects. Plant remains are often present.

scat
2.0 x 0.6 in
5.0 x 1.5 cm

SCAT WIDTH

Habitat: Prefers a mixture of fields and woods. More often found in woodlands than is red fox. Early stage woodlands are preferred, with considerable activity in riparian habitats.

Similar species: Smaller than coyote and wolf. Lacks the ridge of callus on the interdigital pad of the red fox. Differs from coyote in that claws often do not show.

Other sign: Seldom digs dens, but makes use of woodpiles, rock outcrops, hollow trees, and brushpiles. Look for small bones around den entrances.

side trot

climbing tree

front
1.8 x 1.6 in
4.5 x 4.0 cm

no callus ridge

hind
1.7 x 1.6 in
4.3 x 4.0 cm

trot

Kit Fox
Vulpes macrotis

The size of a domestic cat, 3.0 to 5.0 pounds (1.4 to 2.3 kg), with disproportionately large ears. Body color is pale red washed with gray. Tail has a black tip. Swift fox (*Vulpes velox*), a closely related species, is found in the northeast part of the region covered here.

Track: Small for a canid. Claws often do not show. Front foot larger than hind.

Trail: Walking stride 14.0 inches (35.0 cm). Loping stride 22.0 inches (55.0 cm). Dainty trail often mistaken for that of a cat. Details of footprint seldom register in sand.

Scat: Usually has a tapered tail. Scat consists mostly of small mammals and insects, but occasionally birds and reptiles.

front
2.0 x 0.6 in
5.0 x 1.5 cm

SCAT WIDTH

Habitat: Found in sand habitats of the desert or plains where vegetation is sparse and short.

Similar species: Smaller than coyote, whose claws show better. Lacks the ridge of callus on the interdigital pad of the red fox. Tracks may be smaller than gray fox, although distinction may be difficult, but the sand habitat is a good clue.

Other sign: Dens in burrows in the ground, where it hides during the day.

front
1.7 x 1.5 in
4.3 x 3.8 cm

lope

— no callus ridge

hind
1.3 x 1.2 in
3.3 x 3.0 cm

walk

FRONT TRACK LENGTH

FRONT TRACK WIDTH

Coyote
Canis latrans

Collie-size canid, 20.0 to 25.0 pounds (9.0 to 11.0 kg). Male larger than female. Color varies from completely gray to tan to rust. Long, pointed ears and long, narrow muzzle.

Track: Claws usually present. One lobe on the leading edge of the interdigital pad. Inside toe slightly larger than outside. Front foot larger than hind.

Trail: Trotting stride averages 39.0 inches (100.0 cm). Often uses a trot with body turned to the side, leaving a 2 x 2 track pattern. Often lopes, leaving a C-shaped pattern.

Scat: Varies from pure black animal protein to mostly hair with some bones. Tips tapered into long tails.

Habitat: An animal of the open brush country, the coyote digs its den on exposed hilltops or ridges with a view of surrounding area. Where persecuted, may den in a more secluded location.

Similar species: Even adult track is smaller than that of a wolf pup. Track may overlap in size with red fox, but lacks callus ridge

scat
3.0 x 0.8 in
7.5 x 2.0 cm

SCAT WIDTH

of red fox. Track larger than gray fox, and usually shows claws. Differs from bobcat by showing claws and by having one lobe on leading edge of interdigital pad.

Other sign: Marks territory with urine and scat piles. Scat pile locations may be used repeatedly. Uses feet to scratch near scat piles, spreading odor from scat and foot glands to identify territory.

**scratch marks
near scat pile**

lope

front
2.5 x 2.35 in
6.3 x 5.8 cm

hind
2.25 x 1.9 in
5.7 x 4.8 cm

side trot

FRONT TRACK LENGTH

FRONT TRACK WIDTH

Bobcat
Felis rufus

Size of a collie, weighing 13.0 to 35.0 pounds (6.0 to 16.0 kg). Males larger than females. Overall color reddish to yellowish brown, with dark spots or streaks and whitish underside. Ears have tufts at tips. Back of ears and top of tail tip black. Tail is short or bobbed, about 4.0 inches (10.0 cm) long.

Track: Front track is round or wider than long. Hind track may be longer than wide. Claw impressions are usually absent. Toes form a slight arc and toe 3 leads. The leading edge of the interdigital pad has two lobes. Inside toe distinctly larger than outside toe.

Trail: Walking stride is about 20.0 inches (50.0 cm). Usually walks, but bounds with hind feet placed side by side when chasing prey. Winter trails often show random vertical leaps, perhaps signaling that the bobcat has jumped after a flying bird.

Scat: Tends to be constricted and, if dry, separates at constrictions into segments. Ends usually blunt. Dry scat falls apart. Scat from a fresh kill may form a cord of uniform diameter.

broken constriction

scat
3.0 x 0.8 in
7.5 x 2.0 cm

Habitat: Prefers dense cover of swamps and forests, especially with rocky ledges. Open agricultural land is not used. Rock piles, caves, and high rocky ledges are important for bearing young.

Similar species: Differs from coyote and other canids by lacking claws, having two lobes on the leading edge of the interdigital pad, and having toe 3 leading. Substantially smaller than both lion and lynx.

Other sign: Scent marks made by urine, scat, and anal glands. Scrapes dirt or snow over urine and scat. Scratches from rubbing glands are apparent on snow. Caches food by burying.

walk

**vertical
leap from
hind feet**

bound

walk

leading
toe

two lobes

**claw
marks on
tree**

front
2.0 x 2.1 in
5.0 x 5.3 cm

hind
2.1 x 1.9 in
5.3 x 4.8 cm

FRONT TRACK LENGTH

FRONT TRACK WIDTH

Mountain Lion
Puma concolor

Larger than a German shepherd, with male averaging 145.0 pounds (66.0 kg) and female about 120.0 pounds (54.0 kg). Color gray to red, often called tawny, with whitish underside. Back of ears and tail tip black to brown. Tail is more than half the length of the body. Also called cougar or puma.

Track: Track is diameter of a baseball. Front track round or wider than long, and hind track longer than wide. Claw impressions are usually absent. Toes form a slight arc and toe 3 leads. Leading edge of the interdigital pad has two lobes. Inside toe distinctly larger.

Trail: Walking stride is about 36.0 inches (90.0 cm). Usually walks, but bounds with hind feet placed side by side when chasing prey.

Scat: Scat from a fresh kill may form a cord of uniform diameter with very slight constrictions; ends usually blunt. As the carcass on which a lion is feeding dries out, the lion's scat tends to develop constrictions, eventually falling apart when diet becomes very dry.

scat
4.0 x 1.25 in
10.0 x 3.1 cm

SCAT WIDTH

Habitat: Habitat is that of its main prey, deer. Open woodlands with rock ledges and grass (for deer) preferred. Often found in riparian zones with trees.

Similar species: Track differs from wolf by the presence of two lobes on the leading edge of the interdigital pad, by having toe 3 leading, and by usually not showing claws. Differs from wolverine and bears by having only four toes and large toe inside.

Other sign: Often buries scat by scraping dirt over it with front feet. Scraped ground material may conceal food caches. Male will rake up basketball-size patches of brush and urinate on them to mark home range.

Comments: Breeding populations not known from area. Proof of non-feral or non-escaped animals is needed.

bound

**scraped ground
around scat**

two lobes

front
3.5 x 3.5 in
8.8 x 8.8 cm

leading
toe

walk

hind
3.25 x 3.0 in
8.1 x 7.5 cm

FRONT TRACK LENGTH

Raccoon
Procyon lotor

Stocky, smaller than a collie, with broad head and bushy tail. Male averages 18.0 pounds (8.0 kg) and female 16.0 pounds (7.0 kg). Gray to black overall, with black rings on the tail and a black mask on a white face.

Track: Five slender toes, slightly bulbous on the ends. Feet resemble small human hands and feet. Hind foot has a long, naked heel.

Trail: Walking stride averages 27.0 inches (68.0 cm). Roll of hips during walk causes hind foot to register beside the opposite front print. C-shaped gallop is common.

Scat: Highly variable, but often black, even-diameter cord with blunt ends. Often contains crayfish or fruit. Deposited singly or in dung heaps containing scat from perhaps several raccoons. **May carry a parasite that is fatal to humans. Do not smell scat, and wash hands after touching.**

Habitat: River and stream drainages are prime habitats, but storm drains in cities may also provide refuge. Woodpiles in and around towns.

scat
3.0 x 0.75 in
7.5 x 1.9 cm

Similar species: Differs from bear in having slender toes. Differs from river otter by lack of webbing. Larger than mink.

Other sign: Digs holes in streambanks to get at crayfish. Leaves piles of crayfish skeletons and claws. Digs for worms in lawns.

sign left while fishing for crayfish

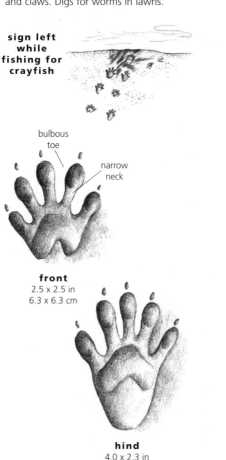

bulbous toe

narrow neck

front
2.5 x 2.5 in
6.3 x 6.3 cm

hind
4.0 x 2.3 in
10.0 x 5.8 cm

gallop

walk

FRONT TRACK LENGTH

FRONT TRACK WIDTH

Weasels
Mustela species

Long-tailed weasel
M. frenata

Three species, with long, slender bodies, varying in size from a regular to a foot-long hot dog. Pointed, flat skull with small ears. Males up to twice as large as females. Largest males weigh about 1.0 pound (0.45 kg). Overall color is brown, with a white belly. In winter, northern individuals turn entirely white. Hairy, slender tail. The small least weasel (*M. nivalis*) lacks the black tip on the tail found in the ermine (*M. erminea*) and the long-tailed weasel (*M. frenata*, shown here).

Track: Wide track. Five toes, in 1-3-1 grouping. Little toe, on inside of foot, often does not register. Interdigital pad chevron-shaped. Heel seldom shows. Difficult to distinguish among species.

Trail: Galloping stride varies from 8.0 to 30.0 inches (20.0 to 75.0 cm). Side-by-side tracks, when examined closely, show one track slightly in front of the other—a gallop. In snow, a drag mark may be found between front and hind prints, sometimes forming a dumbbell shape.

Scat: Long, slender cord, usually with black, toothpaste-like animal protein or hair. Cord tends to fold back on itself. Tapered at both ends.

folded back ⸺

scat
1.5 x 0.1 in
3.8 x 0.3 cm

tail

SCAT WIDTH

Habitat: Prefer dense, low ground cover to open areas. Found in habitats where their prey, rodents, occur in high densities. Trails often lead from one rodent den to another. Travel in snow and ground burrows of other mammals.

Similar species: Differ from other mustelids by their smaller size and the drag mark commonly located between twin track patterns in the snow.

Other sign: Routes seldom follow a straight line, often having many sharp turns. Scat often deposited on raised objects.

erratic route

dumbell shape

weasel trail

foot drag

gallop

front
0.5 x 0.6 in
1.3 x 1.5 cm

proximal pad

heel not included in track measurement

hind
0.6 x 0.7 in
1.5 x 1.8 cm

2 x 2 lope

FRONT TRACK LENGTH

FRONT TRACK WIDTH

Badger

Taxidea taxus

Border collie–size, with flat body, long hair, and long, shovel-like claws, about 18.0 pounds (8.0 kg). Male 25 percent larger than female. Color varies from silver-gray to yellowish brown on back. Belly white. Feet are black or dark brown. White stripe down nose with black markings on sides of face. Short tail.

Track: Diameter of a golf ball, with long front claws, nearly as long as rest of footprint. Five toes, in 1-3-1 grouping. Little toe, on the inside of foot, sometimes does not register. Interdigital pad chevron shaped. Proximal pad often shows. Front footprint larger than hind.

Trail: Walking stride averages 14.0 inches (35.0 cm). Walking is most common, but trotting, with a stride of 29.0 inches (74.0 cm), occurs frequently.

Scat: Seldom found because deposited below ground in burrows. Similar to, but smaller than, coyote scat, without tapered ends.

scat
3.0 x 0.8 in
7.5 x 2.0 cm

blunt ends

hole with dirt mound

Habitat: Open grasslands preferred. Areas with large populations of prey, which includes ground squirrels and prairie dogs.

Similar species: Differs from all other species by long claws on front foot and disproportionately small hind foot.

Other sign: Fresh excavations of large amounts of dirt from burrowing rodent holes indicates hunting activity, especially if excavated material includes large clods or rocks. Freshly widened burrow entrances may have a slightly elliptical shape. The presence of coyote and badger tracks together indicates cooperative hunting.

long prominent claws

front
2.5 x 2.0 in
6.3 x 5.0 cm

proximal pad

heel not included in track measurements

hind
1.75 x 1.75 in
4.4 x 4.4 cm

lope

walk

FRONT TRACK LENGTH

FRONT TRACK WIDTH

Mink
Mustela vison

Size of a small domestic cat, but slender, 1.5 to 3.5 pounds (0.7 to 1.5 kg). Male 10 percent larger than female. Pointed, flat skull with small ears. Overall color is dark brown, with white spots on chin and chest. Hairy, slender tail. Webbing occurs between the toes.

Track: Five toes, in 1-3-1 grouping. Little toe, on the inside of foot, sometimes does not register. Webbing shows between toes in tracks; look carefully. Interdigital pad chevron-shaped. Proximal pad may show in front footprint. Heel seldom shows.

Trail: Bounding stride averages 14.0 inches (35.0 cm). Bounds more than weasels, but a gallop, averaging 20.0 inches (50.0 cm), is also common.

Scat: Long, slender cord, usually tending to fold back on itself. Black or brown in color, occasionally with hair. Tapered at both ends. Often contains remains of fish or crayfish. May be oily and smell fishy. Fish oil keeps scat composed of fish scales from falling apart until oil evaporates, then scales scatter on the ground.

tail

folded back

fish bones

scat
2.0 x 0.25 in
5.0 x 0.6 cm

SCAT WIDTH

Habitat: River- and streambanks. Seldom far from water.

Similar species: Differs from other small mustelids by having more webbing between toes. Larger than weasels. Use of aquatic habitat is an important clue for separation from marten. Tracks and trail much smaller than those of otter.

Other sign: Mink make "post offices," repeated scat deposits on logs exposed above water's edge. Strong, musky, almost skunklike odor from anal scent glands.

fast walk

front
1.7 x 1.8 in
4.3 x 4.5 cm

web

proximal pad

web

hind
1.8 x 1.9 in
4.5 x 4.8 cm

bound

FRONT TRACK LENGTH

FRONT TRACK WIDTH

River Otter
Lutra canadensis

Body and tail form a
4-foot-long cylinder
that tapers to a hairy,
pointed tail. Weight
varies from 10.0 to 30.0
pounds (5.0 to 14.0 kg).
Male slightly larger than female. Overall
color a rich, dark brown, with silver-brown belly. Webbed
toes on front and hind feet.

Track: Large webbed foot is diagnostic, but
look closely because webbing may be difficult
to see. Hind foot is very wide. Five toes, in 1-3-
1 grouping. Little toe, on the inside of foot,
sometimes does not register. Interdigital pad
chevron-shaped. Proximal pad often shows.
Hairless heel on hind foot.

Trail: Walking stride averages 19.0 inches (48.0
cm). Loping stride averages 32.0 inches (80.0
cm). Loping gait patterns are usually turned to the side.

Scat: Usually contains fish remains, including scales and verte-
brae. The texture is oily and the smell fishy. Fish oil keeps scat
composed of fish scales from falling apart. Scat decomposes as oil
evaporates, eventually falling into a pile of scales.

fish parts —

scat
5.0 x 1.0 in
12.5 x 2.5 cm

SCAT WIDTH

Habitat: River- and streambeds. Lives and nests in bank burrows, but may also nest in log jams. In spring, travels overland, often several miles from water sources.

Similar species: Differs from other species by webbing and large, wide hind foot.

Other sign: Loose dirt banks show where otters have rolled to dry off. Rolls around tufts of grass, twisting them into scent posts. Travels by sliding down banks and along level snow and over ice-covered lakes.

tail drag

side lope

webbing

proximal pad

front
2.5 x 3.0 in
6.3 x 7.5 cm

web

hind
3.0 x 3.6 in
7.5 x 9.0 cm

bound

FRONT TRACK LENGTH

FRONT TRACK WIDTH

Striped Skunk
Mephitis mephitis

Black-and-white mustelid, size of a domestic cat, with triangular head. Weight varies from 4.0 to 10.0 pounds (2.0 to 5.0 kg). Male is slightly larger than female. Flat, wide, bushy tail with white hair on top. Long, curved claws for digging.

Track: Half dollar–size, with long front claws. Hind track looks like a little human footprint. Five toes, in 1-3-1 grouping. Little toe, on the inside of foot, sometimes does not register. Interdigital pad chevron-shaped. Proximal pad often shows. Hairless heel on hind foot.

Trail: Walking stride averages 12.0 inches (30.0 cm). Meanders and stops often when walking, leaving extra footprints in trail. Lope may be turned to the side or straight forward.

Scat: Cylindrical with blunt ends. Lacks the long taper and tendency to fold back on itself of other mustelid scat. May be composed entirely of insect parts.

blunt

scat
5.0 x 0.75 in
12.5 x 1.9 cm

fanged puncture

chewed eggs

Habitat: Not habitat-specific. Lives where burrows, cavities, or tunnels are present, including in and around buildings. Presence of insects and small mammals is critical to habitat selection.

Similar species: Differs from other species by having long, wide claws on the front foot. Smaller than badger, with front and hind feet similar in size.

Other sign: Smell of skunk musk identifies nests and burrows. Tears apart nests of small mammals. Bird eggs show four fang punctures around larger hole in shell.

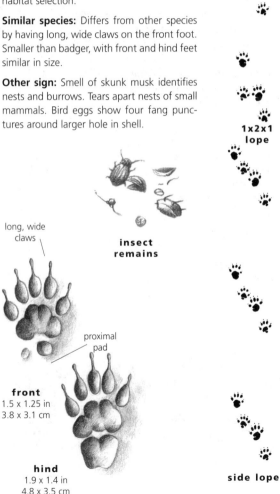

1x2x1 lope

insect remains

long, wide claws

proximal pad

front
1.5 x 1.25 in
3.8 x 3.1 cm

hind
1.9 x 1.4 in
4.8 x 3.5 cm

side lope

FRONT TRACK LENGTH

FRONT TRACK WIDTH

Cottontail Rabbit
Sylvilagus species

Small rabbit with large ears and feet, but small white tail. Averages about 3.0 pounds (1.4 kg). Color pepper-and-salt or gray and white. Two species of cottontail are found in the region. The tracks of these species are indistinguishable from one another.

Track: Toes asymmetrical around foot axis. Track indistinct because the foot is completely haired and lacks pads. Occasionally claws will register; these may be the only sign of a hopping rabbit. Hind footprint about two and a half times longer than front.

Trail: Hopping stride is about 3.0 feet (90.0 cm). Most of the time rabbits hop, but walking patterns will occasionally be observed.

Scat: Dry scat is a slightly flattened sphere. Produces a black, semiliquid scat that is usually re-ingested to utilize remaining nutrients.

scat
0.2 in
0.5 cm

chewed branch and bud

SCAT WIDTH

Habitat: Found wherever there is grass for food and suitable cover, including brushpiles, herbaceous and shrubby vegetation, and grasslands. May use dens of other animals for escape cover.

Similar species: Differs from snowshoe hare by having shorter heels and smaller overall size.

Other sign: Sharp incisors cleanly cut herbaceous vegetation at the height of a sitting rabbit, 4.0 to 8.0 inches (10.0 to 20.0 cm). Look for tips of branches with young sprouts chewed off. The cottontail's bed, known as a *form,* is a shallow depression in earth, grass, or snow.

walk

**claws only
on hard
ground**

hop

claw

toe
position
asymmetrical

front
1.25 x 1.0 in
3.1 x 2.5 cm

hind
3.5 x 1.0 in
8.8 x 2.5 cm

FRONT TRACK LENGTH

FRONT TRACK WIDTH

Jackrabbit
Lepus townsendii (white-tailed) and
L. californicus (black-tailed)

**Large, slender hare with
long ears and feet. Averages
about 5.0 pounds (2.0 kg).
Body color is gray and
white to black and white.
White-tailed jackrabbit
(*L. townsendii*), illustrated
here, has white tail,
and may turn white in the winter.**

Track: Toes asymmetrical around foot axis. Track indistinct because foot is completely haired and lacks pads. Occasionally claws will register, and may be the only sign of a footprint. Hind footprint may be up to three times longer than front. Hind print of white-tailed jackrabbit averages about 10 percent longer than black-tailed.

Trail: Galloping stride may reach 10.0 feet (3.0 m). Tends to gallop rather than bound.

Scat: Dry scat is a slightly flattened sphere. Produces a black, semiliquid scat that is usually reingested to utilize remaining nutrients.

scat
0.3 in
0.8 cm

SCAT WIDTH

**sharp cut
grass**

Habitat: Inhabits open areas. Black-tailed is found in arid regions with sparse grass and desert vegetation. White-tailed is found from plains grasslands to above tree line in the mountains.

Similar species: Track differs from cottontail by having long shape. Differs from snowshoe hare by its narrow width.

Other sign: Sharp incisors cleanly cut herbaceous and woody vegetation. The jackrabbit's nest, known as a *form,* is a shallow depression, usually found under protective cover.

toe
position
asymmetrical

front
1.7 x 1.4 in
4.3 x 3.5 cm

hind
5.0 x 1.5 in
12.5 x 3.8 cm

gallop

FRONT TRACK LENGTH

FRONT TRACK WIDTH

Thirteen-lined Ground Squirrel
Spermophilus tridecemlineatus

Size of a small rat, 0.25 to 0.5 pound (110.0 to 220.0 g). Body is light to dark brown with thirteen white stripes or rows of spots. White belly.

Track: Front print has four toes, with 1-2-1 grouping. Hind has five toes, with 1-3-1 grouping. Toes relatively slender. Front footprint size of a quarter. Hind heel is hairless and may register clearly in track. Long claws may show, especially in front tracks.

Trail: Bounding stride averages 20.0 inches (50.0 cm). Uses a half bound, characteristic of its terrestrial life style.

Scat: Small, usually unconnected ovals.

burrow entrance

scat
0.1 in
0.3 cm

SCAT WIDTH

Habitat: The only ground squirrel of the region, it is found in grassy areas including pastures, and lawns of cemeteries and golf courses of western Pennsylvania.

Similar species: Claws longer and feet smaller than those of tree squirrels. Smaller than wood-chuck.

Other sign: Extensive burrow systems with a labyrinth of entranceways and galleries. Entrances are well hidden in vegetation and seldom have dirt at the entrances.

front
0.75 x 0.6 in
1.9 x 1.5 cm

hairless heel, not
included in track
measurement

hind
1.0 x 0.75 in
2.5 x 1.9 cm

bound

FRONT TRACK LENGTH

FRONT TRACK WIDTH

Woodchuck
Marmota monax

Size of a domestic cat, 5.0 to 10.0 pounds (2.2 to 4.5 kg). Ears and head are short and broad. Tail about one-third body length. Color frosted brown to yellowish brown on back, but paler on belly, dark feet.

Track: Front foot size of a silver dollar, with four toes in 1-2-1 grouping. Five toes on hind foot, 1-3-1 grouping. Toes relatively slender. Four joined interdigital and two proximal pads on front footprint, and four joined interdigital pads on hind foot. Heel is hairless.

Trail: Half bound stride varies from 15.0 to 40.0 inches (38.0 to 100.0 cm). A ground dweller, the woodchuck uses a half bound. Walking stride is 18.0 inches (45.0 cm).

Scat: Rare to find because it is deposited in latrines within tunnel systems. Wide variety of forms, from oval pellets to long cords, all of which may be tightly stuck together. Sometimes lacks defined shape, being dark and runny when deposited.

scat
0.5 x 0.25 in
1.3 x 0.6 cm

Habitat: Open or brushy areas, especially around rocky ravines and cultivated fields.

Similar species: Largest of the squirrels, its track dwarfs other ground squirrels. Track left when drinking at a stream may be distinguished from beaver's by lack of webbing and by having only four toes on front prints.

Other sign: Extensive tunnel system with two or more round-oval openings 5.0 to 7.0 inches (12.5 to 18.0 cm) in diameter. While some openings may have a large mound of dirt, others, excavated to the inside, may not have a mound and be more concealed. Fresh dirt indicates occupancy, if height of burrow exceeds 8.0 inches (18.0 cm), it may have been taken over by red fox.

— proximal pad

front
2.2 x 1.8 in
5.5 x 4.5 cm

hind
2.8 x 2.0 in
7.0 x 5.0 cm

bound

FRONT TRACK LENGTH

FRONT TRACK WIDTH

Chipmunk
Tamias striatus

Slightly larger than a large mouse, up to 3.0 ounces (80.0 g). Reddish fur, with white stripes bordered by black stripes along the sides of the face and body. Haired tail.

Track: Front foot size of a nickel, with four toes in 1-2-1 grouping. Five toes on hind foot, 1-3-1 grouping. Toes relatively slender. Claws short. Hind heel is haired and details are difficult to detect.

Trail: Bounding stride averages 7.0 inches (18.0 cm). Mostly terrestrial, it usually uses a half bound, though full bounds may be observed in its trails.

Scat: Small, usually unconnected ovals.

scat
0.1 in
0.3 cm

SCAT WIDTH

Habitat: Deciduous forest and brush areas.

Similar species: Smaller than ground and tree squirrels. Lacks the long claws of ground squirrel. Smaller than woodchuck.

Other sign: Seeds and nuts of various plants, chewed open on one side.

front
0.5 x 0.4 in
1.3 x 1.0 cm

furred heel, not included
in track measurement

hind
0.7 x 0.6 in
1.8 x 1.5 cm

bound

FRONT TRACK LENGTH

FRONT TRACK WIDTH

Eastern Gray Squirrel
Sciurus carolinensis

Large squirrel, weighing up to 1.5 pounds (0.7 kg). Grayish black with some brown in summer. Belly is whitish. Light-colored ring around eye. Tail is bushy, bordered with white hairs.

Track: Front foot size of a half dollar, with four toes in 1-2-1 grouping. Five toes on hind foot, 1-3-1 grouping. Toes relatively slender. Claws relatively short. Haired hind heel is indistinct in tracks.

Trail: Bounding stride ranges from 24.0 to 36.0 inches (60.0 to 90.0 cm). Straddle 5.0 inches (12.5 cm). Tends to use a full bound.

Scat: Small, shapeless black masses to small, usually unconnected ovals.

scat
0.25 in
0.6 cm

SCAT WIDTH

Habitat: Hardwood forests and river bottoms. Nut-producing trees in territory.

Similar species: Larger than chipmunk. Lacks the long claws of ground squirrel. Larger than red squirrel and smaller than woodchuck.

Other sign: Nests in tree holes and builds twig-and-leaf nests in branches of trees, about 25.0 feet (7.6 m) from the ground.

hind
prints on
front

slow bound

front
1.6 x 1.0 in
4.0 x 2.5 cm

hairless heel, not
included in track
measurement

hind
2.6 x 1.4 in
6.4 x 3.5 cm

full bound

Red Squirrel
Tamiasciurus hudsonicus

Medium-size squirrel, weighing up to 0.5 pound (0.25 kg). Reddish brown back, separated from white underparts by a black stripe. White ring around eye. Slight ear tufts. Tail is bushy.

Track: Front foot size of a quarter, with four toes in 1-2-1 grouping and five pads. Five toes on hind foot, 1-3-1 grouping and four pads. Toes relatively slender. Claws relatively short. Haired hind heel is indistinct in tracks.

Trail: Full bounding stride averages 24.0 inches (60.0 cm). Walk and half bound when searching for food.

Scat: Small, shapeless black masses to small, usually unconnected ovals.

scat
0.4 x 0.2 in
1.0 x 0.5 cm

chewed cones and seed casings

Habitat: Boreal or northern coniferous forests, mixed hardwood forests, and swamps. Infrequently found in deciduous forests.

Similar species: Larger than chipmunk. Lacks the long claws of ground squirrel. Smaller than gray squirrel and woodchuck.

Other sign: Builds twig-and-leaf nests in branches of trees, about 15.0 feet (5.0 m) from the ground. Piles, called *middens,* of pine and hemlock cone scales where squirrel removes scales to get at seeds. Cones are cached 12.0 inches (30.0 cm) deep in the midden for use as winter food. Stripped buds of spruce trees scattered along forest floor.

claws

pads distinct

front
1.2 x 0.75 in
3.0 x 1.9 cm

hind
1.8 x 1.0 in
4.5 x 2.5 cm

hind
prints on
front

slow bound

full bound

FRONT TRACK LENGTH

FRONT TRACK WIDTH

Southern Flying Squirrel
Glaucomys volans

A small squirrel, weighing 4.0 ounces (112.0 g). Its silky fur is olive brown on the back and lead gray on the underside. A fold of skin stretches between front and hind legs and body, forming a wing and allowing the squirrel to glide. Its bushy tail is flattened to aid in sailing.

Track: Front foot size of a quarter, with four toes in 1-2-1 grouping. Five toes on hind foot, 1-3-1 grouping. Toes relatively slender. Claws relatively short and may not show. Hind foot interdigital pads form a tight crescent, though proximal pads are lacking.

Trail: Bounding stride averages 20.0 inches (50.0 cm). Uses a full bound.

Scat: Small, usually unconnected ovals.

Habitat: Deciduous and coniferous forests, though often found in attics of houses.

scat
0.1 in
0.3 cm

wing marks

SCAT WIDTH

Similar species: Differs from all other squirrels and chipmunks by the tight crescent of interdigital pads on the hind foot. Lacks the long claws of ground squirrels. Smaller than woodchuck.

Other sign: Skin flap outlines may show in dust or snow. Sometimes builds roof on bird nest to use as den. Tree dens may hold twenty squirrels during the winter.

hind prints
on front

front
0.5 x 0.5 in
1.3 x 1.3 cm

bound

interdigital pads
arrayed in a
crescent shape

hind
1.5 x 0.5 in
3.8 x 1.3 cm

wing
drag

FRONT TRACK LENGTH

FRONT TRACK WIDTH

Plains Pocket Gopher
Geomys bursarius

Guinea pig–size rodent with minute eyes and ears and a short tail. Has external, fur-lined cheek pouches.
Averages about 12.0 ounces (340.0 g), with males larger than females. Yellowish brown to dark, almost black. Two distinct grooves down front teeth.

Track: Five toes front and hind foot. Toes are relatively slender. Front feet have relatively long, wide claws for digging. Claw length is equal to or longer than toe length. Good tracks are seldom found and more data are needed on track size. Measurements are approximate.

Trail: Walking stride is 6.0 inches (15.0 cm).

Scat: Thick, short cords.

Habitat: Needs deep sandy soils preferably associated with grasslands, meadows, and fields.

Similar species: Differs from other rodents by large, wide claws.

scat
0.2 in
0.5 cm

SCAT WIDTH

Other sign: Summer mounds consist of loose dirt forming a flat mound with no entrance visible (gophers close the tunnel as they go back underground). Winter casts of soil and rocks show where gophers packed dirt into snow tunnels while they burrowed for food. Scats are often found in the tunnel casts.

front
0.8 x 0.7 in
2.0 x 1.8 cm

hind
1.0 x 0.7 in
2.5 x 1.8 cm

fast walk

walk

FRONT TRACK LENGTH

FRONT TRACK WIDTH

Ord's Kangaroo Rat
Dipodomys ordii

Stocky and mouse-size, about 2.0 ounces (56.0 g), with large hind feet and long fur-tipped tails. Reddish brown on back, white side stripe, and dark belly.

Track: Hind foot has four toes. Long heel on hind foot may register. Feet are furred and toes difficult to distinguish.

Trail: Bounding stride averages 7.0 inches (18.0 cm) and typically ranges from 8.0 to16.0 inches (20.0 to 40.0 cm). Often bounds on hind feet only. Tail drag often observed.

Scat: Small, usually unconnected, ovals.

Habitat: Low-elevation animal. Prefers sandy soil where it can easily dig burrows.

scat
0.2 in
0.5 cm

SCAT WIDTH

Similar species: Track differs from western jumping mouse by greater width and more hair. Bounds on the hind feet only; no front prints visible in the bounding pattern.

Other sign: Scrapes out shallow "bathtubs" in dust as it dusts itself for protection against fleas.

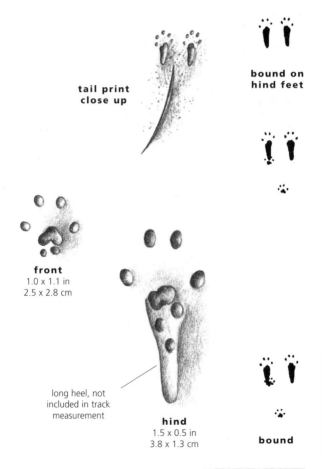

tail print close up

bound on hind feet

front
1.0 x 1.1 in
2.5 x 2.8 cm

long heel, not included in track measurement

hind
1.5 x 0.5 in
3.8 x 1.3 cm

bound

FRONT TRACK LENGTH

FRONT TRACK WIDTH

Plains Pocket Mouse
Perognathus flavescens

Small mouse, weighing 0.3 to 0.6 ounce (8.0 to 16.0 g). Body color is mixed yellowish and brown. Hair is soft. Tail as long as or longer than head and body. Fur-lined, external cheek pounches.

Track: Track about dime-size, though more data is needed. Four toes on front foot. Five toes on hind foot. The foot is hairy and prints are often indistinct.

Trail: Bound stride is about 4.0 to 6.0 inches (10.0 to 55.0 cm). Uses a half bound.

Scat: Oval-shaped pellets similar to those left by house mice.

Habitat: Prefers sandy soils with short grass and other sparse vegetation.

scat
0.1 in
0.3 cm

SCAT WIDTH

Similar species: Differs from other mouse and vole species by indistinct track and occasional tail drag. Differs from shrews by having only four toes on front feet. Smaller than other rodent tracks.

Other signs: Burrows lack mounds. Stores caches of seeds often in depression on the ground surface

indistinct print

front
about 0.25 x 0.25 in
0.6 x 0.6 cm

hind
0.5 x 0.4 in
1.3 x 1.0 cm

FRONT TRACK LENGTH

FRONT TRACK WIDTH

Deermice
Peromyscus maniculatus

Small mouse, weighing up to 1.0 ounce (28.0 g). Adults are reddish brown to brown on back with a white belly, while juveniles are dark gray on the back with a light gray belly. Large eyes and ears. Tail is long and haired.

Track: Track smaller than a dime. Four toes on front foot, in 1-2-1 grouping. Five toes on hind foot, 1-3-1 grouping. Four joined interdigital and two proximal pads on front footprint; five joined pads and heel on hind footprint. Heel is hairless.

Trail: Bounding stride averages 8.0 inches (20.0 cm). Those species that use a full bound are climbers and nest in grass, shrubs, or trees. Those species using a half bound nest on or below ground. Both types occasionally trot. Tail drag may be present.

scat
0.1 in
0.3 cm

SCAT WIDTH

Scat: Oval-shaped pellets similar to those left by house mice.

Habitat: Ubiquitous, being found from deserts to the northern tree line, from below sea level to the top of high peaks.

Similar species: Differs from shrew by having only four toes on the front feet and by being slightly larger. Differs from vole by often showing a tail drag and by most often bounding. Lacks the long heel of the jumping mouse. Smaller than chipmunk.

Other sign: Compact grass nests without entrances may be found under logs, rocks, and boards. Enters and exits through the grass wall, which closes up after passage. Caches large quantities of seeds in any convenient protected area. Leaves feces near and in nest.

tail drag

4 x 4 bound

3 x 3 bound

front
0.3 x 0.3 in
0.8 x 0.8 cm

hind
0.4 x 0.3 in
1.0 x 0.8 cm

FRONT TRACK LENGTH

FRONT TRACK WIDTH

Eastern Woodrat
Neotoma floridana

Size of a house rat, weighing about 10 to 16 ounces (280 to 450 g). Head gray, sides light brown; feet and belly are white. Densely haired long tail is white below and dark gray above. Back gray to reddish, belly and throat white to light gray. Large naked ears and long whiskers on face.

Track: Four toes with 1-2-1 spacing on front foot and five with a 1-3-1 on hind foot. Toes relatively slender, and toe pads slightly constricted. Three joined interdigital, one remnant, and two proximal pads in front footprint and three interdigital palm pads and two proximal pads on hind print.

Trail: Bounding stride is 16 inches (40 cm) and walking stride is 6 inches (15 cm). Bounding is probably the most common gait, but woodrats also frequently walk.

Scat: Small oval pellets.

Habitat: Limestone caves, cliffs, talus slopes and residual sandstone boulders in beech, poplar, and maple forest. Uses abandoned buildings, especially outhouses.

scat
0.2 in
0.4 cm

nest

SCAT WIDTH

Similar species: Larger than mice and voles. Differs from squirrels by the presence of heel pads on hind foot.

Other sign: Bulky houses may contain two or more nests. Houses are made from dry grass, shredded bark, fur, feathers, and twigs. Caches of food, including nuts, berries, foliage, and mushrooms, may be found on nest. Nearby post-office latrines on rocks may be used by several individuals, creating 2-inch (5-cm) deep masses of scat.

front
0.7 x 0.6 in
1.8 x 1.5 cm

constricted pad

remnant pad

heel not included in track measurement

hind
1.5 x 0.9 in
3.8 x 2.3 cm

bound

fast walk

FRONT TRACK LENGTH

FRONT TRACK WIDTH

Voles
Microtus species

Many species of mouse-size mammals, related to lemmings and weighing up to 3.0 ounces (80.0 g). ***Microtus* species, here represented by the meadow vole, *M. pennsylvanicus,* are gray to gray-brown on back, with a light-colored belly. Small, stocky mammals with short ears and small eyes, almost hidden by their fur. Short tails are sparsely haired.**

Track: Track smaller than a dime. Four toes on front foot, in 1-2-1 grouping. Five toes on hind foot, 1-3-1 grouping. Four joined interdigital and two proximal pads on front footprint and four interdigital pads and one proximal on hind footprint. Heel is hairless.

Trail: Trotting stride 6.0 inches (15.0 cm). Usually trot, seldom bound. Tails usually do not show in the trail.

Scat: Oval-shaped pellets similar to those left by house mice, often piled in tennis ball–size latrines that may hold hundreds of pellets.

Habitat: *Microtus* species are grass-loving species, found near

scat
0.1 in
0.3 cm

SCAT WIDTH

latrine

meadows across North America and north to the Arctic.

Similar species: Differ from shrews by having only four toes on the front feet. Differ from mice by seldom showing a tail drag and by most often trotting. Lack the long heel of the jumping mouse.

Other sign: As snow melts in the spring, grass nests lacking entrances may be found. Snow melt may also reveal 1.0-inch (2.5-cm) cords of grass and debris, stuffed into snow tunnels during the winter to make space elsewhere in the tunnel network. Vole latrines are usually found near nests, while mice leave feces near and in their nests. Worn runways through the grass.

bound

fast trot

front
0.3 x 0.3 in
0.8 x 0.8 cm

hind
0.4 x 0.3 in
1.0 x 0.8 cm

five pads
only

heel not included in
track measurement

trot

FRONT TRACK LENGTH

FRONT TRACK WIDTH

Meadow Jumping Mouse
Zapus hudsonius

A small—about 0.8 ounce (25.0 g)—mouse with long hind feet and long, sparsely haired tail. Yellowish sides, darker brown back, and white belly. White tip on long tail.

Track: Four toes on front foot, in 1-2-1 grouping. Hind foot is about the size of a quarter, exceptionally long and narrow, and has five toes in 1-3-1 grouping. Toes relatively slender. Heel is hairless.

Trail: Bounding stride 60.0 to 120.0 inches (150.0 to 300.0 cm). Makes sharp turns during travel. May cover considerable distance per stride when pursued. Tail drag often observed.

scat
0.1 in
0.3 cm

SCAT WIDTH

Scat: Small oval pellets.

Habitat: Mountains, seldom found more than 3.0 feet (1.0 m) from a stream.

Similar species: Differs from other rodents in having long, narrow hind feet and tail drag. Differs from kangaroo rat by bounding from all four feet, not just hind.

Other sign: Small piles of grass stems left after eating. Round grass nests.

tail drag

front
0.4 x 0.25 in
1.0 x 0.6 cm

long toes

heel not included in track measurement

hind
1.0 x 0.25 in
2.5 x 0.6 cm

bound

FRONT TRACK LENGTH

FRONT TRACK WIDTH

Muskrat
Ondatra zibethica

Large, ratlike, stocky, up to 4.0 pounds (2.0 kg). Males slightly larger than females. Small eyes and ears. Tail is black, flattened, scaly, with few hairs.

Track: Four toes on front foot (small fifth nubbin may show in very clear tracks) and five on hind foot. Toes very slender. Hind foot appears wider than long.

Trail: Walking strides average 11.0 inches (28.0 cm). May lope with body turned to side.

Scat: Oval, at most three to four times longer than wide. Often deposited in a sticky mass on exposed logs at water's edge.

Habitat: Marshes and lake edges, secondarily on streambanks. Large rivers are not as frequently used. Cattails and rushes predominate.

Similar species: Differs from beaver by smaller size and lack of webbing. Differs from mink by long slender toes and by usually walking.

scat
0.2 in
0.5 cm

SCAT WIDTH

Other sign: Small conical domes made from reeds serve as dens. Cut grass and reeds near water's edge mark feeding sites. Muskrats make "post offices," repeated scat deposits, on rocks.

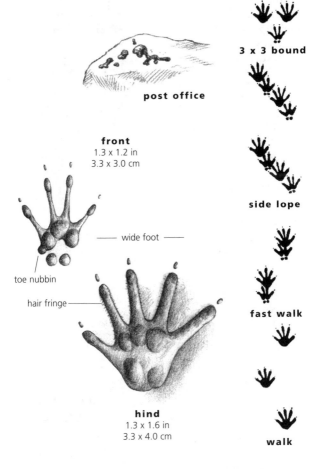

4 x 4 bound

3 x 3 bound

post office

front
1.3 x 1.2 in
3.3 x 3.0 cm

side lope

wide foot

toe nubbin

hair fringe

fast walk

hind
1.3 x 1.6 in
3.3 x 4.0 cm

walk

FRONT TRACK LENGTH

FRONT TRACK WIDTH

Prairie Dog
Cynomys species

Blacktail prairie dog
C. ludovicianus

Size of a large guinea pig,
2.0 to 3.0 pounds (1.0 to 1.4 kg).
Fat, yellowish brown ground
squirrel. The blacktail prairie
dog (*C. ludovicianus*) has a
black-tipped tail, the whitetail
(*C. gunnisoni*) a white-tipped
tail. Lives in large colonies.

Track: Size of a quarter dollar.
Long claws on front prints for digging. Four toes on front track, in 1-2-1
grouping (toe 5 does not show). Five toes on
hind track, 1-3-1 grouping. Toes are relatively
slender.

Trail: Bounding stride averages 30.0 inches
(75.0 cm). Uses a half bound. Trots more than
other squirrels.

Scat: Ranges from oval to a cord five to six
times longer than it is wide. Scats are often
connected by narrow filaments.

scat
0.1 to 0.2 in
0.3 to 0.5 cm

mound and hole

SCAT WIDTH

Habitat: Prairie and open grassland, where colony's "town" may consist of thousands of acres of low dirt mounds concealing tunnels.

Similar species: Differs from ground squirrel by the presence of longer digging claws. Claws longer and broader and feet smaller than those of tree squirrels. Smaller than marmot. Larger than mouse and vole.

Other sign: Colonies consisting of many burrows with elevated mounds and manicured "lawns" of grazed grass.

side lope

long claws

front
1.0 x 0.8 in
2.5 x 2.0 cm

narrow toes

hind
1.0 x 0.9 in
2.5 x 2.3 cm

bound

FRONT TRACK LENGTH

FRONT TRACK WIDTH

Beaver
Castor canadensis

Largest rodent in North America, 30.0 to 60.0 pounds (14.0 to 27.0 kg). Distinguished by large, webbed hind feet and large, horizontally flattened tail. Fur overall is dark brown to almost black, with lighter belly.

Track: Front and hind prints show five toes. Hind foot may be larger than a human hand. Webbing between hind toes shows, but only when pulled tight by splaying of toes. Clear tracks are difficult to find, as the hind foot steps on the front foot and the dragging tail obliterates many prints.

Trail: Walking stride 18.0 inches (45.0 cm).

Scat: Seldom found, as they are usually deposited in water, where they disintegrate quickly. Marshmallow-size, a little longer than thick. Consist of wood chips.

scat
1.0 x 0.7 in
2.5 x 1.8 cm

wood chips

Habitat: Seldom found far from a creek, river, pond, or lake.

Similar species: Differs from other rodents by large size and webbing. Differs from river otter by long, slender toes and pointed heel, and by lacking a chevron-shaped pad.

Other sign: Dams and conical lodges, built of twigs and sticks. Standing, cutoff tree trunks end in a tapered cone. Debarked tree limbs in the water.

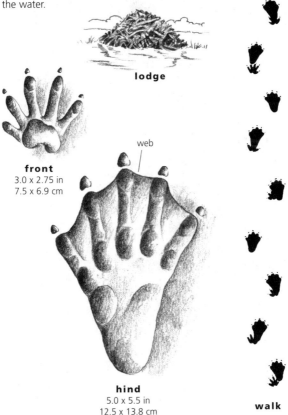

lodge

web

front
3.0 x 2.75 in
7.5 x 6.9 cm

hind
5.0 x 5.5 in
12.5 x 13.8 cm

walk

FRONT TRACK LENGTH

FRONT TRACK WIDTH

Porcupine

Erethizon dorsatum

Basketball-size or larger, 10.0 to 25.0 pounds (5.0 to 11.0 kg). Stocky body, with short legs. Distinguished by the presence of quills. Brown to yellowish brown in color.

Track: Rough texture formed by small nubs on soles of feet. Four toes on front foot and five toes on hind. Toes often do not show. Claws often show.

Trail: Walking stride 17.0 inches (43.0 cm). Tail drag often present.

Scat: Winter scat formed from feeding on conifers is red. Summer scat includes more

scat
0.5 in
1.3 cm

**debarked
stick with
chew marks**

herbs and shrubs and is brown to black. Scat from both seasons may be composed of individual pellets or strings of pellets connected by fibers.

Habitat: Generally found near forests, but may be far from trees if shrubs are available.

Similar species: Rough texture on sole of foot is diagnostic. In snow, trough made by dragging belly highlights its stockiness, separating it from faster-moving mammals.

Other sign: Twigs with bark chewed off, found at the bases of trees. Will perch in a tree for days, chewing the bark, thereby killing the tree.

tail drag

amble

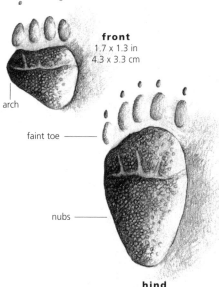

front
1.7 x 1.3 in
4.3 x 3.3 cm

arch

faint toe

nubs

hind
2.7 x 1.7 in
6.8 x 4.3 cm

walk

FRONT TRACK LENGTH

FRONT TRACK WIDTH

Bison
Bison bison

Large member of
the cow family,
with a large
shoulder hump
and massive skull.
Male may weigh
1500.0 pounds
(680.0 kg), female
about 1300.0 pounds (590.0 kg). Head is dark brown to
black, with the rest of the body brown. Calf is red overall.
Both sexes have horns that are never shed.
Horns of the male are larger.

Track: Very large, with round outer walls.
Heavy bulls wear hooves down so much that
the division between clouts may not be readily
observable. Pad at back of clout forms a V.

Trail: Walking stride is 50.0 inches (125.0 cm).
Usually walks, but occasionally lopes. When
stampeding, uses a full gallop, and intergroup
distances may reach 10.0 feet (3.0 m).

pie

stack

scat
"cow pie" diameter 8.0 in
(20.0 cm) or greeater

**female
horn**

**male
horn**

Scat: Usually moist, forming "cow pies" much of the year. Young bison scat appears as a stack of cookie-size wafers.

Habitat: Grassland and open mountain meadows. Nowadays, herds are found only in national and state parks, and on private ranches in some areas.

Similar species: Differs from moose track by having rounded wall outline and rounded tips. Larger than other hoofed animals.

Other sign: The most conspicuous sign of the bison is its wallow, a large depression where both sexes roll around, usually in dry dirt, but occasionally in wet areas.

lope

walk

pad turns up on inside of clout

front
6.25 x 6.75 in
15.6 x 17.0 cm

hind
6.0 x 6.0 in
15.0 x 15.0 cm

FRONT TRACK LENGTH (50%)

FRONT TRACK WIDTH (50%)

Elk
Cervus elaphus

Medium-size, larger than deer, males averaging 700.0 pounds (315.0 kg) and females 450.0 pounds (200.0 kg). Reddish to dark brown, with a yellow rump patch. Males shed antlers annually. Also known as wapiti. Re-introduced in east.

Track: Blocky, with each clout wide at the leading tip. Pad of hoof occupies rear third of each clout; subunguinis occupies remaining two-thirds of each clout.

Trail: Walking stride 52.0 inches (130.0 cm). When chased by a predator, gallops and occasionally pronks.

Scat: Most of the year, scat consists of pellets that scatter on impact with the ground. When the diet is moist, nipple-dimple shape predominates, changing to oval as vegetation dries. When scat is moist, pellets stick together.

nipple

dimple

scat
pellet 0.5 in
pellet 1.3 cm

antler

SCAT WIDTH

Habitat: Forest. Beds in dense trees during the day, moving out into clearings to graze during twilight hours.

Similar species: Differs from deer and moose by having a small pad at the rear of the hoof.

Other sign: Removing antler velvet, bulls strip bark from young saplings and break off limbs, often killing the trees. Height of tree wound shows animal height. Bulls make mud wallows in the fall. During rut, look for areas where bulls have sparred with the ground using their antlers.

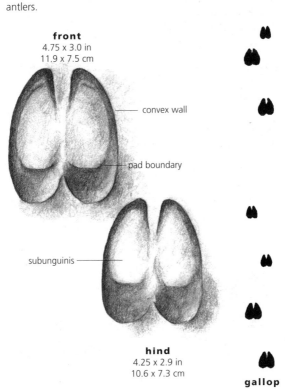

front
4.75 x 3.0 in
11.9 x 7.5 cm

convex wall

pad boundary

subunguinis

hind
4.25 x 2.9 in
10.6 x 7.3 cm

pronk

gallop

FRONT TRACK LENGTH

FRONT TRACK WIDTH

Pronghorn Antelope
Antilocapra americana

Smaller than deer; found only in North America. Male averages 125.0 pounds (56 kg), female about 110.0 pounds (50 kg). White and tan to reddish brown, with black and brown markings on the head and neck. Male has forked horns that are shed annually.

Track: Identified by the concave outline of the wall, which bends slightly inward at a point about one-third of the way back from the tip. Pad is bulbous.

Trail: Ambling stride is 35.0 inches (88.0 cm). Most common gait is an amble, a fast walk where the hind foot registers slightly in front of the front footprint. Often uses a Z-shaped gallop, with a stride ranging from 80.0 to 145 inches (200.0 to 363.0 cm).

scat
pellet 0.3 in
pellet 0.8 cm

paw

urine

scat

SCAT WIDTH

Scat: Typically, well-defined pellets that often stay together upon impact with the ground.

Habitat: Open and shrub country of short- to mid-grass prairie. Herbs and winter browse above the snow are important. Commonly found with sagebrush.

Similar species: Differentiated from deer by its small size and concave wall. Lacks dewclaws.

Other sign: The territorial marking of the male pronghorn is a spud, produced as the male sniffs and paws the ground after urinating and defecating to spread the odor.

gallop

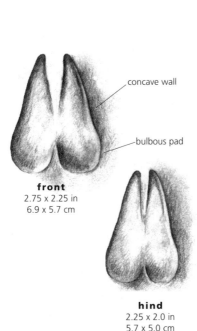

concave wall

bulbous pad

front
2.75 x 2.25 in
6.9 x 5.7 cm

hind
2.25 x 2.0 in
5.7 x 5.0 cm

amble

FRONT TRACK LENGTH

FRONT TRACK WIDTH

White-tailed Deer
Odocoileus virginianus

Smallest member of the deer family. Male averages 130.0 pounds (60.0 kg), female about 110.0 pounds (50.0 kg). Coat is reddish in summer and blue-gray in winter. The prominent white tail is carried erect when animal is disturbed. Antlers, found only on male, have tines, or points, branching off main beam.

Track: Heart-shaped, with convex wall. Pad occupies most of the clout; subunguinis slender.

Trail: Walking stride 30.0 inches (75.0 cm). Pronks or stots with front and hind feet striking the ground at the same time. Gallops when in a hurry.

Scat: Usually dry, falls apart when it hits the ground. Pellets vary from nipple-dimple shape to oval.

scat
pellet 0.3 in
pellet 0.8 cm

antler

SCAT WIDTH

Habitat: Generally closed timber, but moves out to grasslands at twilight to feed.

Similar species: Smaller than elk, has more slender tips, and pad occupies most of clout.

Other sign: Gathers (yards up) in large numbers in sheltered groves during the winter. Breaks off limbs of trees when removing the velvet from antlers. Velvet is difficult to find, as both deer and rodents eat the nutrient-rich material. Height of tree wound indicates animal height.

pronk

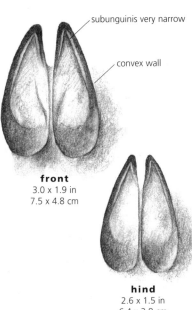

subunguinis very narrow

convex wall

front
3.0 x 1.9 in
7.5 x 4.8 cm

hind
2.6 x 1.5 in
6.4 x 3.8 cm

gallop

FRONT TRACK LENGTH

FRONT TRACK WIDTH

Selected reading

Tracks and tracking

Bang, P., et al. 1972. *Collins Guide to Animal Tracks and Signs.* London: Collins Sons.

Brown, R., J. Ferguson, M. Lawrence, and D. Lees. 1987. *Tracks and Signs of the Birds of Britain and Europe: An Identification Guide.* Kent, England: Christopher Helm.

Elbroch, M. 2003. *Mammal Tracks and Signs: a Guide to North American Species.* Mechanicsburg, PA: Stackpole Books.

—. 2001. *Bird Tracks and Signs: a Guide to North American Species.* Mechanicsburg, PA: Stackpole Books.

Fjelline, D. P., and T. M. Mansfield. 1989. Method to standard-ize the procedure for measuring mountain lion tracks. In *Proceedings of the Third Mountain Lion Workshop,* ed. R. H. Smith, 49–51. Prescott, AZ: Arizona Game and Fish Department.

Forrest, L. R. 1988. *Field Guide to Tracking Animals in Snow.* Harrisburg, PA: Stackpole Books.

Halfpenny, J. C. 1997. *Tracking: Mastering the Basics.* 180 min. A Naturalist's World. Videocassette.

—. 1986a. *A Field Guide to Mammal Tracking in North America.* Boulder, CO: Johnson Books.

—. 1986b. Tracks and Tracking: A "How To" Guide. Gardiner, MT: A Naturalist's World. Slides.

Halfpenny, J. C., et al. 1996. Snow tracking. In *American Marten, Fisher, Lynx, and Wolverines: Survey Methods for Their Detection,* eds. W. Zielinski and T. Kucera, 91–163. General Technical Report PSW-GTR-157. Berkeley, CA: USDA Forest Service, Pacific Southwest Research Station.

Headstrom, R. 1971. *Identifying Animals Tracks: Mammals, Birds, and Other Animals of the Eastern United States.* New York: Dover.

Murie, O. 1954. *A Field Guide to Animal Tracks.* Peterson Field Guide Series, no. 9. Boston: Houghton Mifflin.

Rezendes, P. 1999. *Tracking and the Art of Seeing: How to Read Animal Tracks and Sign.* 2nd Ed. Charlotte, VT: Camden House.

Seton, E. T. 1958. *Animal Tracks and Hunter Signs.* New York: Doubleday.

Recommended field identification guides

Burt, W. H., and R. P. Grossenheider. 1964. *A Field Guide to the Mammals.* Peterson Field Guide Series, no. 5. Boston: Houghton Mifflin.

Conant, R. 1958. *Reptiles and Amphibians of Eastern and Central North America.* Peterson Field Guide Series, no. 12. Boston: Houghton Mifflin.

Jones, J. K., D. M. Armstrong, R. S. Hoffman, and C. Jones. 1983. *Mammals of the Northern Great Plains.* Lincoln: University of Nebraska Press.

Kays, R. W., and D. E. Wilson. 2002. *Mammals of North America.* Princeton, NJ: Princeton University Press.

National Geographic Society. 1983. *Field Guide to the Birds of North America.* Washington, D.C.: National Geographic Society.

Peterson, R. T. 1984. *Birds of the Eastern United States.* Norwalk, CT: The Easton Press.

Sibley, D. A. 2004. *The Sibley Field Guide to Birds of Western North America.* New York, Alfred A. Knopf, Inc.

Stebbins, R. C. 1985. *A Field Guide to Western Reptiles and Amphibians.* Peterson Field Guide Series, no. 16. Boston: Houghton Mifflin.

Index

About the author

James Halfpenny has searched for dinosaur tracks in Colorado and Montana, tracked wildlife in Tanzania and Kenya, studied endangered species on China's Tibet-Qinghai plateau, and researched the polar bears of Hudson Bay and Greenland. Jim specializes in educational, environmentally oriented programs about mammal behavior, tracking, and cold. Since 1961 he has taught outdoor and environmental education for a vast array of schools and organizations, including the Smithsonian, National Outdoor Leadership School, Outward Bound, the Appalachian Mountain Club, The Wilderness Society, National Wildlife Federation, Defenders of Wildlife, and National Audubon Society. He has trained rangers in tracking techniques at Yellowstone, Glacier, Grand Teton, and Rocky Mountain national parks. His research has also taken him to Antarctica, Africa, and Japan, and all over North America. He is a fellow of the Explorer's Club and a Vietnam veteran. Halfpenny was featured, with Australian aborigines, Kalahari Bushmen, and Alaskan Inuit, in a documentary about the loss of native tracking skills shown on the Discovery Channel. He is a past field director for the Long-Term Ecological Research program in the Alpine Tundra and project coordinator for the University of Colorado's Institute of Arctic and Alpine Research. He is also the senior author of the *Scats and Tracks* series, *A Field Guide to Mammal Tracking in North America* (Johnson Books), *Yellowstone Wolves in the Wild* (Riverbend Press), *Discovering Yellowstone Wolves: Watcher's Guide* (A Naturalist's World), *Winter: an Ecological Handbook* (Johnson Books) and *Bare Feet, Wet Socks: Writing about Winter* (edited with Ann Zwinger, Caldera Press). He lives just outside Yellowstone National Park in Gardiner, Montana.

About the illustrator

Todd Telander is a freelance natural science illustrator and wildlife artist. He studied biology and environmental studies at the University of California, Santa Cruz, where he became interested in illustration. His work appears in Falcon's *America's 100 Most Wanted Birds, Birder's Dictionary, A Field Guide to Cows,* and *A Field Guide to Pigs,* as well as in museums, galleries, and private collections. Todd lives in Walla Walla, Washington, with his wife, Kirsten, a writer, and their two sons, Miles and Oliver.